Don't let anyone look down on you because you are young, but set an example for the believers in speech, in life, in love, in faith and in purity.

The Apostle Paul
1 Timothy 4:12

Bridge-Logos

Orlando, FL 32822 USA

FIRE IN THE CORE

A SouthTown Riders Devotional

Edited by Sally Tolentino

Printed in the United States of America.

Library of Congress Catalog Card Number: pending
International Standard Book Number 0-88270-002-2

G163.317.B.m603.35250

A SouthTown Riders Devotional

FIRE IN THE CORE

Edited by Sally Tolentino

Bridge-Logos

Orlando, Florida 32822

CORE SPORTS

Core sports are extreme sports.
While other sports make you lay it on the line, core sports
    demand that you take it over the line.
Engaging in core sports requires that your core is fit and healthy.
By core, we mean the center of your body, soul, and spirit.
Anything less, and you'll never make it.

CONTENTS

INTRODUCTION

Have you ever had a dream so big that the possibility of it becoming a reality was a thought you could hardly entertain? A dream so huge that you knew it would take a miracle for it to ever come true? That was just how the SouthTown Riders came into being. It all began with a young man's dream that in his mind was as improbable as winning the lottery, yet in his heart was so real that he dared to believe the impossible.

And what *was* his dream? It was to have a camp where young people who loved action sports could come and wakeboard, skateboard, or even participate in BMX biking. It would be a place where they would be encouraged to confront their fears as they held on to a tow rope for the first time, or forget their inner struggles as they rocketed down a half pipe; a place where they could gain hope that they too could achieve their goals as they successfully jumped into an "X up" on their bike, and most of all, a place where they could laugh a wholesome laugh. Why? Because just maybe for the first time ever they would realize that they were special people, loved by an awesome God who had a plan and a purpose for their lives, and that they could actually know Him through His son Jesus Christ. This is the dream that would become SouthTown's passion.

Maybe at one time in your life you have also thought, "I could make my dream come true if I just had money!" Well, we, the small group of young men and women who believed in *this* dream, had absolutely none. But that didn't stop us. We began our first camp as a wakeboard camp, with the only facility being the dock of the lake house the guys were renting at the time. An old faded ski boat, some badly worn life jackets, and a couple of used wakeboards made the dream a reality for the fifty participants who came that first summer. The next season, when the number of youth who signed up nearly reached one hundred and twenty, the SouthTown team scrambled to borrow another boat and pooled their meager resources to buy some extra life jackets at Wal-mart. By the end of that second year, we realized that to accommodate the projected number of youth for the following season, we would need more wakeboards, more and better life jackets, and at least two new, smooth running boats. Now that is a costly undertaking and a big order, especially for a group so young that some of us were still in school!

IT ALL STARTED WITH A

So do you give up on the dream? After struggling so hard to get this far, is *this* the point where you say, "It's impossible, there's no way!"? Not at all. This is where faith in God steps beyond the boundaries of mere religion. It is where trust in His Word outweighs the improbabilities. The SouthTown team believed that God had given us the vision for this unique ministry, and so we went to Him in prayer one night and just simply asked for two new boats. However, being the humans that we are, we tried to help God out some by contacting a Christian boat company, hoping this would be the answer. But it wasn't. So we just continued to pray. A short while later through a series of circumstances that we never could have imagined, a company called Skier's Choice gave us the use of two brand new, top-of-the-line ski boats valued at around $80,000 for the camp! Another company, Jet Pilot, supplied the boats with brand new life jackets! And SouthTown had already obtained new wakeboards from Hyperlite! For the corporate world to shower these blessings on such a small group of unknown "visionaries" was truly a miracle. It could have only been the hand of God, and this knowledge greatly impacted our lives as well as the ministry.

Is following a dream as easy as just saying a prayer? Not exactly. The SouthTown team is here to tell you that we have had to "tread some rough water" and "pass through some very hot fire." Lessons in brokenness, obedience, humility, and faith, to name a few, have come at a huge price and are an ongoing schooling process. Yet SouthTown's theme Scripture verse, Isaiah 43:2, sits on top of every boat and can be seen on wakeboards and skateboards, the web site, and in our literature. It says it all.

SIMPLE DREAM.

Dare to dream.
Nothing is impossible with God

"When you pass through the waters, I will be with you; and through the rivers, they shall not overflow you. When you walk through the fire, you shall not be burned, nor shall the flame scorch you. For I AM the Lord your God."

So don't ever be afraid to dream, or be discouraged by those who may not share your vision. Put your trust in the One who is able to make the impossible happen. As you will see in the pages to come, SouthTown's dream continues to unfold with each new day. We invite you to share the experience and enjoy the ride.

The Team (Front row, left to right) Christy Tolentino, Danny Tolentino, Erin Easter, Andy Riese, Meredith Tolentino, David Tolentino. (Back row) Owen Parker, Dawn Parker, Bekah Wood, Mike Wood, Tim Morrison.

I want to learn from everyone else on the team. I also want other people to see Jesus Christ in me through my actions and words, and to be the best I can be as a wakeboarder and for Jesus.

Lauren Hustad, Age 13

SO WHATS WITH THE NAME?

SouthTown Riders. Certainly not the typical name for a youth ministry. So where did it come from?

We guys from SouthTown always wakeboarded in a small cove on the south side of the lake, tucked away from sight of the boats on the main waterway. It was there that we practiced all our new tricks.

There was also a group of wakeboarders that rode on the north side of the lake. These guys found out about our group on the south side and began talking trash about our riding, even though they had never seen us ride.

So one day, tired of the verbal attacks, all of us from the south side decided we would go up to the north side of the lake and show our stuff. That was the end of the northern riders bad-mouthing the southern riders; instead, their mouths dropped open in amazement at what their "rivals" were capable of doing behind a boat.

At about that same time, we were stuck on a song by P.O.D., one of our favorite bands. The song talked about "Southtown," and we made it our name. From then on, we became known and respected on the lake as "The SouthTown Riders." We adopted this name as our official ministry title.

HOW TO USE THIS BOOK

This book is the story of our lives: the young men and women who make up the SouthTown team. Spread throughout are small lessons that we believe are the reflection of what we have experienced in our walk with Jesus Christ. Although it is a devotional, you may choose to read a story, look at the pictures, or read the little "sermons" that come from our discussions around the campfire in any order you wish, and re-read as many times as you like. We're sure that each time you do, you'll gain new insight as to what it really means to live the lifestyle of a "follower of Jesus".

At the end of the book there is some information on how you can become part of the SouthTown community. Check it out. Whether your interest is wakeboarding, skateboarding, or finding a way to use your talents in any area, we at SouthTown are dedicated to helping you achieve excellence in your relationship with God.

Join us on the greatest adventures of our lives.

Believing in Jesus doesn't mean you have to be boring. On the contrary!

Austin Parker, Age 18

Being involved in SouthTown made me want to learn more and more about God because I thought it was cool that wakeboarders were so much into God.

Troy Ogburn, Age 14

DAVID'S STORY

Darkness comes on a daily basis. I mean it always comes every evening when the sun goes down. Besides the passing of the sun below the horizon, the dark also came inside my head. I struggled every day with thoughts of depression and death. I was only fifteen with a fixation on dying.

I lived with both of my parents, which seemed to be a rare situation for kids my age. I had all the material things that I could have wanted: clothes, video games, and other middle school pop culture wants. It wasn't the need of stuff that really got to me; it was the need to be accepted by my peers at school. I mean it was middle school.

My life has its ups and downs like everybody's. But I depend on God to take care of me. David Tolentino

I Wanted
to be Accepted

I was smart, artistic, had long hair before it was cool, and I didn't live in Tega Cay. (That's where all the cool kids lived). That's what got to me, not that I didn't live in Tega Cay, but the fact that I wasn't part of the cool kids' club. Loose associations don't count. I mean passing somebody in the hall and saying, "Hey!" doesn't exactly put you in the inner circle of coolness. I just wandered somewhere in the middle, not part of the popular bunch and not part of the outcasts and geeks. I was just a plain kid who got lost in the crowd.

Where I did stand out was at my church's youth group. People knew my name, and a lot of people even wanted to hang out with me. But for me the church youth group couldn't be my measurement of social acceptance and popularity, because that was easy there. We were supposed to "love one another."

No, I had to be accepted at school, and this need consumed me. Who would think that being cool and accepted at school could mean so much to a person? Just look at where it took the couple of guys at Columbine High School. The pursuit of acceptance turned to anger through distortion and lack of self esteem and self worth. I'm not saying that I was thinking of hurting anybody, but I did become angry. By my eighth grade year of middle school, I had become *very* angry at the students around me. It made me furious that some students would pick on kids just because they had acne or a guy may have seemed a little feminine. It was an everyday experience to hear some insecure boy being called "fag" or "queer" or some girl being called "ho" or "skank" because some guy was telling stories about a make-out session or getting to "third base."

What set me off was when the verbal attacks started to come my way. I started getting called "fag" and "gay" because I liked art and dance and theatre. Yet, these name-callers were so quick to forget that I was an all-star baseball player and a presidential fitness award winner. I was a huge athlete; it's just that I didn't play basketball and football. I guess if you didn't make a school team then you just weren't recognized.

I know that it doesn't only come down to sports, but it's also what you do outside of school with people that puts you on the "cool" list. What party you showed up to and what music you were into. I wanted to hang with those people so bad at those parties, but mom and dad just wouldn't let me be involved with any questionable activity. If someone's mom and dad weren't there and they hadn't talked to them, I wasn't going to be a part. In retrospect, I can understand why they did this, but during the time I just wanted to be part of the accepted crowd.

My Parents Were Strict

My parents even regulated the music that I listened to. Every lyric was under scrutiny to make sure that evil things weren't trying to enter my mind. If the CD or tape didn't come from the Christian book store, they weren't going to hand the money over. I used to look for every little word in a song that would mention God, and say, "Look, this band knows God. See, they said His name." I didn't care if they used cursing or swearing, *I was just looking for justification to fulfill a need*, and wanted to be listening to what everybody else was listening to. I didn't know the music everybody was talking about, and hadn't been to all the concerts, and didn't have one of those t-shirts that you could only get at a show. I was out of the loop, and I got called out on my lack of knowledge and ignorance in pop culture.

The Forgotten Middle

I was slipping further and further into the group of the forgotten middle. My mind was constantly fighting a battle with what I was feeling and what was really happening. I remember sitting in my room with my door locked, just sitting in my bed crying. I had no idea why. I see now that frustration had taken over, and I was pinpointing people in my life that I could blame for my current condition. Anger was being spawned in my heart; death was speaking in my ear.

Suicide Plans

I was lying in bed when the idea of suicide first came to me. I was staring at the ceiling, with one of those constant glares that if you look long enough, the images before you become blurred. I concentrated and was fixated on the

shadows that lie in the corners of the room. I pretended that they were moving, and they were moving closer and closer to me until finally darkness was all I saw. I was trying to imagine what the feeling of death would be like. It was a kind of mental preparation. I was defeating my fear of dying by trying to mentally experience the consuming darkness of the mind shutting down.

I saw suicide not as a plan to escape life because of inner pain or self-pity, but as a way of getting back at the people who had wronged me. I thought it would be the ultimate way to get noticed. It would cause those people to feel guilty for the things that they had done to me, without the chance of ever asking my forgiveness. It is almost like being a martyr: giving my life up to fight against a certain group of people.

This way of fighting back can only be done with a heart that has been implanted with deep anger. Anger and hate can cause war; it can also move a man to kill himself as justification for wrongs he feels.

So, I began to plan my death, a death that would take place in front of the people who hurt me every day of my life, my middle school peers, the same ones who committed crimes against the geeks and castaways.

My First Encounter with God

When I was fourteen, the year before all of this turmoil, I had my first physical encounter with God. I was healed miraculously of a damaged nerve leading into the back of my brain.

I had been playing basketball one afternoon with one of my best friends, Jesse. He was a far better player than I was. We were really getting worked up in an intense game of "twenty-one." Of course, he was winning and I was playing catch-up. I would try the most ridiculous shots, just hoping to score a basket while he was guarding me. I was attempting a turnaround jump shot when the seizure hit without warning. As I leaped into the air, I felt an intense heat shoot through the right side of my arm. Then a tingling sensation started in the right side of my tongue. Different sensations were bombarding the entire right side of my body. As my feet came back down to the pavement, I lost total control of my entire right side. It was completely paralyzed, down to my tongue. I remember trying to stand up, but the only things that worked were my left arm and leg. I felt like an animal that had been hit by a car, struggling to stand up and move itself off to the side of the road where it would later die. The sensations lasted for about 30 seconds. Jesse just looked at me in silence, not knowing what to do, stricken stiff with fear. The episode subsided and I regained feeling and mobility. What did I do? I continued to play basketball and pretend as if nothing had happened. It wasn't exactly the smartest thing to do, but it made me classify the seizure as nothing outside of normal. My friend did not ask questions; he just went on playing, and it became one of the quietest basketball games ever played.

This "paralyzing" occurred another three times before I decided to tell my parents. They freaked out and couldn't believe that I hadn't told them. It was straight to the doctors for me. Fear began to materialize in my head. I asked myself, "What if they tell me that something is majorly wrong? What if they tell me that I can never play sports again?" The questions just ran through my mind and disturbed me to the point of tears. There I was—14 years old and thinking about losing all ability to have fun. It wasn't like a person who gets injured in a car accident, where they are instantly forced to deal with the new ailment, where there's no option and they just have to cope with it. For me it was the anticipation of what the doctors would say. It killed me to think of their response because on the outside, it seemed like I was perfectly okay, but on the inside, something was seriously wrong.

The first set of neurological tests was brief, typical, and non-threatening: "Follow my finger with your eyes, and stand on one foot with one hand out." Who

knows what that stuff tells them, but it was more strange than scary. But when I told the doctor what had been happening, a look of concern overtook his face. I remember him taking his hand and placing it on the back of my neck. It's weird that to this day, I still remember that his hands were so cold and that they had that "freshly-been-washed-30-times-in-one-day" smell. The doctor pressed softly into the back of my neck, and knew that something was not right. He told me that the blood veins going to my brain felt peculiar and that he would like to take a MRI of my neck. He said that my condition was serious.

What he said next destroyed my self-esteem, and made intangible fears a reality. He said that I was not to do any more physical activity. Sports were out of the question. He told me that I was to do nothing more strenuous than walking. He even considered placing me in a wheel chair till the tests were done and the results were in, just to make sure. I was outraged at this, of course. I refused that idea. Then he told me why. He said that the vein in the back of my head was damaged, and as a result certain actions would cut off the blood flow to that portion of my brain.

The reason for the paralyzing effect had now been determined. However, he said that I was lucky that the seizures' effects up to now had not been permanent, but that the next one could prove to be deadly. "To be deadly"… I'm only 14 and I could die? Why, God, are you doing this to me? How can you love me and let this happen to me? I've been going to church. I even went on a mission trip. So, this is what I get in return. Some God you are. Ruin my life. Why am I even alive? WHY AM I EVEN ALIVE?!?"

Knowing I Might Die Drove Me to Live

That is when I decided to take up core sports (extreme sports). I had always liked inline skating, but now I was going to go all out against doctor's orders. I would go jump off ledges and sets of fourteen stairs. I would practice 360s and 540s off of my parents' porch. I even got a ramp to jump the back end of my brother's truck. I was just waiting for the seizure to take place. I told my parents that If I was going to die, I might as well die having fun living my days to the fullest. I wasn't going to let some doctor tell me what I can do and can't do! Skateboarding became a habit. I knew that if I was going to get hurt, I might as well be doing something that is worthy of getting hurt. And I did get hurt. There went the vein again. Back on the ground with the numb tongue. What was I thinking? Was the rebellion worth this? I told no one.

I Didn't Care; I Had No Control

The week before the scheduled MRI, I dealt with reality. The last couple of weeks were spent believing a lie that I didn't care about life and death. It's amazing how your mind can tell you a lie for so long and then it just seems like overnight that it becomes truth. Something was seriously wrong. I was going to have to have surgery. The doctors were using the MRI as a map to go in and work on that vein. I didn't want that at all. Here was the kid who was going to rebel and go out with a bang, and now a surgery is going to scare him to tears.

I had no control of the situation. I thought I was in the hands of the doctors, but I really was in the hands of God. He knew the outcome for my life, and I didn't. It was that last day before the MRI that I came to the grips with God for the first time. I would trust the God of my parents to be the God of my life also. I had knowledge of God and the amazing things that He had done for my parents and their missionary journeys, but how much is mere knowledge worth when you need a miracle?

My Youth Pastor Shows Up

The day of the MRI, I remember standing outside in the lobby of the hospital. The floors were marble and the reflections were intense from the sun beaming in through the entrance windows. Time was slowing down and minutes began to seem like hours. The agony was unbearable, waiting for my time to go into the examination room. It was in those long moments that my youth pastor, Daryl Sutherland, walked in the front door of the lobby. He came over to me and simply asked how I was doing. Then he took me to the side and told me that he had come there to pray for me. I was so grateful that someone else besides my parents cared enough to even show up to be with me, that I could have cared less about the prayer part. And of all people, it was my youth pastor, the man who I lied to all the time, cussed at behind his back, and thought was just one of those pastors who were obligated to the kids only when there was an event. That day he showed me the love of Christ. Going out of his way to find the kid in the corner who wasn't the perfect one, but seeing that he had great potential.

"Jesus, be with David as he goes into the doctor's office. Give him strength and let him feel peace as he walks out today in knowing that You are taking care of him." It was the next thing that hit me hard as he placed his hand on the back of my neck, "Jesus, You died to save us and You died to heal us of our infirmities. Heal this boy and show him that you are a God who is real and a God who loves him." I was thinking to myself, when is he going to throw that part in about, "God, if it is Your will, let him be healed, and if it is not, we will accept that also." Nope. No cop out tag line at the end of this prayer. Just the firm statement backed up by faith that Jesus would heal me. I felt nothing. Nothing special happened, no extra warm fuzzies running down my spine. Nothing. Same feelings as before now it was just a closer time for me to go into the machine.

MRI and a Miracle

I was laying on my back in the white cylinder with earplugs to help drown out the loud clicks and bangs of the MRI. All I could see were my toes through a small perfectly angled mirror that was strategically placed on a frame that went around my head to prevent claustrophobia. It would be an hour and a half that I could not move. What am I going to do for that time? Think about girls, sing to myself in my head. The possibilities of the imagination are so endless when you're just laying perfectly still in a really loud white tube with only you and your mind. It was in this hour and half that I realized that it wasn't only me and my mind present in that machine. I believe I had one of my first real conversations with God. In that conversation, I told Him that if He healed me, I would give Him all the glory and worship Him with my body. I would play music, dance, compete, skate ... all as acts of worship, and give the credit to the God who loved me enough to heal me. Where did that statement come from? Desperation. I was at one of the lowest points in my life and I needed hope. The only place I felt I had to turn was to God. I knew that He had heard me, and I walked out of that testing session with a peace in my heart that all would be okay.

The following weeks were spent doing the regular things a teenager does. Soon we would be notified of the outcome of the testing. When we did finally receive the results, they showed that nothing was out of the ordinary in the back of my head! No vein out of place! All the things that the doctor had been concerned

about were proven nonexistent by the results of the MRI. What a relief to me and my parents that I wouldn't need major surgery.

Yet once it was over, I passed off this news almost like the whole entire experience was so trivial. I lessened the importance of what had happened in my mind so that I didn't have to give God the credit that He deserved, or live up to the things that I had said to Him while I was in the MRI. I testified with my mouth that God had healed me, but in my heart I had almost become unmoved by what God had done. Don't get me wrong. It wasn't because of bitterness towards God. It was just that this seemed to me like just one more thing in the list of things I knew He had done in the past for my parents. It was a head knowledge of who Jesus was and His abilities, and I played head games with what had happened. I know part of my heart *wanted* to truly accept this miracle, that God had actually listened to my prayers and answered them, but my mind won over, and so life went on as usual with an increased capacity for the alternative sports, now that I was living a one hundred percent healthy life again.

Back to Suicide Planning

It was entering into my eighth grade year of middle school that my mind started entertaining those thoughts of death and suicide. I was starting to feel depressed, I say the "feeling" of depression because on the outside I was sure not to let anyone know what was going on the inside. I wanted so badly to be fully accepted by my school peers. I was so tired of being in the middle. I wanted to be on top for a change. I tried, I failed, and I put on the mask that everything is just okay. It was the same cover-up that everyone uses to make

Progressive Edge

To achieve a progressive edge, you should cut out away from the wake, then turn into the wake and increase your cut more and more as you approach the wake.

the outside world think that nothing's wrong. It's when internal turmoil starts to become too great for the container it exists in, that it explodes and produces unbelievable results. It's the reason people say, "How could he do that? Everything seemed okay. He was just an ordinary kid." It is this inner turmoil where hope alone brings peace and calms that unwieldy inner being. Some people see that hope in drugs, some in violence, some in sex, some in hate, some in suicide; all these outward actions are used as an escape, in hope that the inner pain and suffering will go away.

I remember walking to my mom's school after I got out of classes for the day. At that time my mom owned a small after-school Spanish school. Her school gave students not in high school the opportunity to learn the growing American language of Spanish. I walked this walk every day. Sometimes I would walk alone, and sometimes with people I thought were friends. These people who walked with me were double-sided. Because when we walked down the street, they were my friends. We talked, we laughed, and we had a lot in common. It is as if we had been the best of friends. Yet that was all the friendship seemed to last, the walk after school.

Now don't take it as I was one of those kids with absolutely no friends. I had friends… they were all just part of the "middle group" in middle school life. I had acquaintances with the popular kids. I just wanted to be accepted into their ranks, and in middle school, acceptance doesn't come often. Middle school had to be the hardest social proving ground in adolescent life.

What started the anger and hurt feelings was when I had the chance to be with one of the popular kids alone, like on the walk home. It seemed like friendship and acceptance was easy then. The problems came when the people that I thought I had become friends with got together in the group. It became ruthless. It was almost as if I didn't exist. I remember getting picked on by some of the guys, and looking toward the people that I thought had befriended me, and they would do absolutely nothing. Worse, in their struggles for acceptance, they would also join in the bashing. How shallow we are in need of acceptance. We'll destroy anybody to make ourselves just feel a little bit better. The shallowness killed me inside. It made me mad. It also destroyed a little piece of me that brought my self worth down just a notch every time this happened.

This is when my plot for revenge started. I would plan to destroy the people who hurt me. Not by physical actions, but mentally showing them who they were. To show them that they pushed me to this, and they had destroyed so many others. The plan was to glorify myself through death. My death would bring all the attention to me. Yes, let them cry over me, let them feel sorrow, let them wonder what could have driven me to this, let them feel the pain of guilt. I would make them realize that I existed no longer ... and it was because of them. I would be giving them a taste of what

Middle school had to be the hardest social proving ground in adolescent life.

they had been doing to me, but on a far more massive scale. I just remember the words constantly going through my head, "I'll show them! I'll show them!"

I can't say that I created the means for the suicide; I was inspired by an individual who I still remember to this day. It wasn't going to be the regular shoot yourself, slit your wrist, overdose on painkillers, and hang yourself kind of self-pity death. In my seventh grade year, there was this girl who would walk down the yellow lines in the middle of the street. She was doing it for the attention, not as a death wish, just to freak people out. She was an outcast, part of the group nobody talked to. Part of the group on the bottom of the social scale. She was considered a loser because of her economic status. She was just a poor girl from the other side of the tracks. A nobody. But when she walked in the street, she became somebody; she was noticed. She had the attention of everybody walking home on the sidewalks, and all the students who were getting picked up by their parents from school. It was the main road to and from the entrance of the middle school, the perfect stage for such an act. The kids yelled at her and the cars honked for her to get out of the middle of the road. You could see her thriving on the attention.

I thought to myself, "If she can get that kind of reaction just walking in the middle of the street, what kind of reaction would she get if a car hit her? How about if the car hit me? Everyone would expect someone like her to do it, but not me." This would be no accident. It was set. That was how I would die—on display in front of those people who walked home with me, on display for the whole school to witness. The best part is that the place where I was going to do it would be in front of a church.

You made a promise to me,

I started the planning process in my room. I'd lie on my bed and stare at the ceiling. Preparations must be taken so that everything would go smoothly. I'd have to make sure that the car that would hit me would do the job. I didn't just want to be maimed for life. I wanted the impact to take care of it. I decided that it would have to be a truck. The place would also be important; it couldn't be on a curve where the speed would be too slow. It would have to be on a straight portion of the road. The only place for that was right in front of the church. On my walks home from school, I walked *now totally alone*. Why alone? I took mental notes of the cars that passed by. I did this for a couple of weeks. My vehicle for destruction had been chosen. It was a brown and tan Ford Bronco with brush guards and really big tires. I chose the Bronco because it would always be speeding down the road, the faster the better. The Bronco was driven by a high school student who would pick up his younger sibling after he got out of school. I saw the Bronco every day; the time of its arrival became predictable to the point that I could get the timing perfect: I would arrive at the place that I needed to be when it would be coming down the street.

Putting the Suicide into Motion
It was that day. The time had to come. I gave no clues to family or friends about what I was about to do. I had played the part that all was fair and well in my life, and that I was content with my life how it was. School was long that day. It seemed that the day was never going to end. I didn't really talk to anyone unless they talked to me first. I just sat and thought about what I was going to do that afternoon. It finally came. The hour of judgment had come to pass. David was going to stop time that afternoon for everyone. I watched the clock as school let out, knowing that my window of opportunity would be small. I started the walk down the street. I was so anxious I could hardly control myself.

I would walk with people and make sure that I would walk off the sidewalk, just a little in the street. One foot on the curb and one foot on the road. I stepped back on the sidewalk and started walking a bit faster so that I could get in front of everyone and make sure I had some time to meet the Bronco. I passed the curve in the road, and there it was—the Bronco at the far end of the street, just turning onto the street. Could timing be any more perfect? I would be able to meet the vehicle right at the point that I planned. I got myself ready. I walked a littler slower and a little closer to the road.

I took two steps out into the empty road and started walking. It was now or never. My stand had been made. The preparations followed to the mark. I was now in front of the church and the Bronco was within 100 feet, traveling fast towards me.

God Gets Between a Good Suicide Plan and a Bronco

"What are you doing?! I did not heal you so that you would end your life like this. You made a promise to me, and you will keep it!" In a split second, my mind raced with all the faces of the people who truly loved me: my parents, my family, my brother, my sister, my youth pastor, and a couple of friends at youth group. A swarm of emotions came over me. I felt like I had betrayed all those people who really loved me. I was destroying their lives and they would never understand why I did this to them. Was the need to be popular that important? Why did I need to make this point? Will my "popular peers" not just destroy themselves on their own? I looked up and the Bronco was still coming. It was almost as if God was screaming at me, "I am the one who loves you, I am the one who has already walked this street for you! Get off that street now!" At

that moment, I felt like I was pushed to the side. I looked up and the Bronco was within feet, and I was suspended in time, not on the street, but now on the sidewalk. The Bronco just passed by. I was left standing there, looking at the church. I looked at no one. I just walked the rest of the way by myself in tears. I sat outside my mom's school, cleared up my eyes, and prepared myself to act like nothing had happened. I ended up not staying with my mom; I got one of the parents of the Spanish students to take me home that day. That was that. I moved on without question, but without coming to God ... just yet.

Life Begins to Change

It was in these next couple of months that my methodology for living started changing. It was New Years Eve and my youth pastor had invited me to the youth group's party. He told me to bring my bass guitar because there would be some other guys there who would be playing guitars and stuff, and I would probably like to meet them and play with them. I walked in that night and mingled. Nothing special really happened. I met up with the guys playing guitars; we chilled and talked about music and forming bands. I was the only bass guitarist there, so I was needed by the other guys who played. No band is complete without a bass. Maybe this night would turn out good after all.

Then a guy walked through the front door with a big black guitar shaped bag on his back. Great. It was a bass guitar. There went my chances to play with these guys. I thought, "He'll probably show me up in under five minutes."

I didn't even talk to the guy the whole night. The clock struck midnight, and it was time to go home. I had arranged a ride home with a friend earlier that night. The irony of the situation got to me. It turned out that my ride was giving this bass guitar guy a ride home also. I found out in the car when I had to sit beside him. We started with small talk, moved on to personal interests, and by the time we got dropped off, we had clicked. It turned out that Kevin would soon become my best friend, and still is to this day.

We played music together, rode to church together, hung out, skated, played video games. If we were going somewhere or doing something we were probably going to do it together. It was mid-February, and a youth trip to Gatlinburg, Tennessee was coming up called "Transformation." It was an annual trip for our youth group. I invited Kevin to come along for the fun. I couldn't have cared less what the services were like at this spiritual renewal weekend. I just liked going there because it was a place to meet girls, and it was like a carnival in the mountains. Tons of fun cheesy stuff to buy with mom and dad's money. Kevin seemed to be taking the nightly services more serious than I was. I just looked on, went with the flow, and waited for the nights to be over. But Kevin was really intense about was what going on in the services. I remember him going up to the front when the speaker made the call. I just stood at my seat and watched the passing of time.

Something happened to Kevin that weekend with God. Something that had not yet happened to me. We both grew up in Christian family homes, so he knew about God and Jesus just as much as I did, but there was just something different about Kevin. His entire temperament changed. He was just happy with life; he even wanted to go to church more than we had to. He started reading his Bible … and actually using the thing! I just carried one around to make sure I had the look down. What stuck out to me the most was when Kevin took all his CDs and broke them in half. He said that all this stuff just brought him down, and he didn't need that anymore. Something really had happened to him! Maybe God really did do something in his life at Transformation. Did He save him? That is so relative. Save him from what? I asked Kevin what had happened. He told me about how he used to get depressed and how he couldn't take people picking on him. He also told me that before we had met, he had also had a suicide plan. He was going to jump from a twenty foot concrete wall face first into the cement below. It was at the back of the church that we attended. He went on to tell me how God had spoken and talked to Him that weekend in the mountains, and that He accepted that Jesus would be his Lord. He said that ever since then, things had been different in his life.

Filling the Hole in My Life with Music and God

I now knew what I *really* wanted. Not just a healing to make it better, but a change in hope. I wanted the hope that Kevin had: a hope in God that would allow true joy in life to be achievable. That's all we're really looking for in life. It's that hole in our soul, that need for something to hope in. This time I wanted to fill this hole with God instead of myself, anger, and other frivolous destructive substitutes.

Kevin invited me to visit a church in Florida where his dad would be playing the drums for the weekend. I knew when he asked me that this trip would be different, because I could feel the want to change my life, and have that newness and hope that God had given Kevin. The church we would be visiting was a church that was experiencing the outpouring of the good news of God, Jesus dying to free us from sin, with the evidence of thousands of people coming and making the commitment of placing Jesus as Lord of their lives. These people were being changed. There were stories of drug addictions, depression, all the things that would destroy a human, being totally removed from their lives when they placed their faith and hope in Jesus Christ. These people were being saved from themselves. I too now wanted this salvation.

The Night It All Came Together

It was the first night of services for that weekend. I had just gotten to my seat with Kevin. I remember being nervous and excited all at the same time. I don't even remember what the speaker talked about, but by the time he was finished, I was in tears and knew that I needed God to be the Lord of my life, not just a God who I asked for stuff, but a God who I wanted to serve. He had been calling me all these years. I just hadn't been able to see the hope He had for me. I had built up walls because I didn't want to let God in. Now was the time. At the end of the message, the speaker made the call for people to come down to the front and place ourselves at the mercy seat of God. He said that God's grace was enough to forget the wrongs that we had done. That God wants to take care of us. It would be as simple as making Him Lord. That we needed to come and believe that Jesus is Lord, that He died and rose up from the dead, and that through this, we could be bought by His shed blood to be reunited with God.

As I moved forward, I remembered everything that I had done to God, and I immediately felt convicted of all those things that I told Him I would do when I was in the MRI. I felt convicted for turning my back on Him so many times before. I felt convicted for knowing the truth about God for so many years and never turning to Him to be my God. My response to all this was to ask forgiveness of all these wrongdoings. And unlike anything I had ever experienced before, I felt peace in my soul. I can't even put the words to describe the feelings of my past being taken away from me. I had been forgiven. The forgiveness was evidence that God had saved me. My old life was just that—my old life. I had been freed of all that pain and anger that I had carried around inside of me. I felt so accepted that I didn't need anybody else to accept me but God. That is what I had been looking for the past couple of years at middle school. Now I had found the acceptance not in the people around me who didn't love me, but in the God surrounding me who had always loved me.

After that portion of the service was over, the church got together and prayed for the people who came down. Me included. The person who prayed over me was a little old lady. The last thing I remember her saying is that God had a plan for my life. Then it was as if everyone disappeared from the room. It was almost as if God turned the lights off and played a movie on the wall in front of me. I watched myself skating and snowboarding. But there were all these other kids with me, and I was leading them through the streets and down the mountain. That movie stopped and then another one started. It was of me dancing on a theatre stage. That one ended and another started. This time I was speaking in Spanish, sharing what God had done for me to a whole bunch of kids. That one ended and the last one started. It was of my family and me; we were all working together. We were working with youth. It wasn't at a church, but there were skate ramps and all kinds of activities. There were kids just having fun, and we were there with them. I saw all the things that I had promised God that I would do to worship Him, and more.

I woke up from the movies, and felt like God had just told me what I was supposed to do with my life. I would serve Him through all those things that He had shown me. Through the sports, arts, and working with youth. Looking back, I see now that God was starting the preparations for SouthTown, to pass on the Hope of Jesus Christ through nontraditional means. Not through preaching at a church, but by being examples and giving testimony to what God had done for us, using all the talents that He has blessed us with.

Never the Same

Life has never been the same since that day that Jesus became Lord and saved me. Life has been exciting and good, but it hasn't just been a "walk in the park." What do I mean here? My life has its ups and downs like everybody's. But I depend on God to take care of me, and have the assurance that He loves me with an unconditional love that frees me from pain and hopelessness. He has always been there, letting me know He is there. I walk in true joy. My hope is in Him.

DAVID TOLENTINO

Who is God?

Have you ever found yourself wondering, "Who is God?"
Well, so have I … along with every other person who has walked
the face of the earth. I would like to answer that question with one
word: **LOVE**.

You may be saying to yourself, "Come on, Shawn. Love? Could you
possibly be any more general than that?" Or better yet, "God is
love, yeah right—like he has ever showed me even the slightest bit
of love."

Just think about it; I'm not talking about the kind of love that you feel
for a car or a nice pair of jeans, or at least some things I claim to
love. I'm talking about a deep love that you will die for, a love that
would drive you to go to war and die for what is right, a love that
would compel you to take a bullet in the head for the cause you so
strongly believe in, a love that would lead to a cross to be mutilated
and crucified in order to redeem the very same people who begged
for your execution. God is that LOVE! That kind of love has given
people the heart to do the things for thousands of years above and
much more than I could ever dream of.

For so many years I looked at God as being this scrooge of a judge
with a 2x4 waiting for me to step out of line so that He could whack
me across the knees with it. Or maybe you have seen God as
nothing more than a cop riding your tail, watching you squirm, just
waiting to flash those pretty blue lights. It's really ironic because He
is quite opposite. He is the Dad standing at the end of the driveway
with sobbing eyes and open arms waiting on his screw-up son, who
wasted all of his inheritance and self-respect, to return home. He is
the young woman who shaves her head so that a little girl with
cancer can have the hope of looking normal. He is also the person
who hugs an AIDS patient infested with sores because they have not
felt human arms wrapped around them in years.

Are you getting the point? "Who is God?" was never intended to be
a complicated question or even a question at all. We all know who
God is; it's just a matter of coming to the realization that He is
surrounding us, always has been, and most importantly, always will be.

Now you have the answer to this age-old question, and you can do with it as you wish. I chose to accept it and in doing so, I began to search for God's ultimate act of love. It didn't take me long to find it. I'll give you one big hint as to who it is: Jesus Christ. Now it's your duty to discover the ultimate act of God's love for yourself, and if I may suggest it, the Bible is a good place to start. May all of your heart's deepest desires be fulfilled in your pursuit of LOVE.

Shawn Redmond

Pleasing God in whatever you do is a great goal to shoot for.

Tim Holford Age 14

Success is not what you've done, but what you've allowed God to do.

So You Call Yourself a Christian?

When people think of Christianity, a couple different stereotypes come to mind. One is that Christianity is based on participation in the institution of the church. Can you believe it? How much you show up to church! In fact, some Christians claim that title because simply "showing up" defines a Christian instead of a personal relationship they could have with Him.

Being from the Bible Belt, I can tell you that this definition of Christian describes a large portion of the population. If participation in Sunday morning worship or Wednesday night youth group allows you to enter into relationship with God, then almost everybody in the South is "going to heaven."

But that's wrong. While it's true that *religion* is practiced on Sunday and Wednesday, Christianity is a lifestyle every day.

The other stereotype of Christianity is that all Christians are hypocrites. Why is this stereotype even in existence? Because Christians proclaim what they do and don't do. So when they mess up and go against what they proclaim they do or don't do, they are held accountable by other people watching with scrutiny. So, when you say what you do and don't, you are automatically, instantly a hypocrite.

The amazing fact is that this general population is where the name "Christian" came about. What am I saying? In ancient days, the days when Jesus walked the earth, a group of people not part of the discipleship of Jesus actually brought about the name "Christian" to describe followers of Christ. They were from the city of Antioch (Acts 11:26). This city wasn't exactly built on the teachings of Jesus. Actually, Antioch was more of a pagan-based social structure.

Implications of a non-believing society naming the believers "Christians" are tremendous. What are the implications? Well, Scripture suggests that there was a large group of believers there.

They must have made such an impact on the surrounding population that a name for these followers of the Messiah had to be given. Thus, the name "Christian" was placed on them. Was it because they went to church? Absolutely not. They were recognized because they stood out. Did they have to go around proclaiming that they were Christians? No. They lived lives that reflected the teachings and lifestyle of Jesus Christ, so they were named followers of Christ (the definition of Christian), a suitable title for this population of believers.

If you live your life by example, in relationship with Christ, and don't just practice religion, you truly have a light inside you that will burn brighter than, "I went to church this Sunday." If someone recognizes that you're a Christian, that's far better than your saying it. Plus you'll instantly defeat the stereotype of hypocrisy because you haven't told anyone what you do and don't do, but have shown them with your lifestyle.

At SouthTown we try to lead our lives through example. Sure, sometimes we proclaim who we are and make mistakes, but we just want other people to see that we are "Christians" instead of us having to tell them. This is how we try to do it: "Love the Lord your God with all your heart, with all your soul, and with all your mind. This is the greatest and most important commandment. The second is like it: You shall love your neighbor as yourself" (Matthew 22:37-39).

CORE ACTION

Take note if someone you don't know recognizes you as a Christian without your having to say it. What did you do that gave it away? How did the other person let you know that he was on to you?

DANNY'S STORY

My body lost all power to stand. The cold floor of my apartment reached up and viciously grabbed my swirling head as I crashed. But the floor didn't break my fall. I continued through the tile, falling helplessly into the darkness of another world, trapped in the evil claws of a huge crusher. With every pounding beat of my heart, it squeezed me tighter and tighter, until I was terrified that my very life would soon be just a memory in someone's photo album.

For the first time in my life, I had my own encounter with God, and I would never forget it. Danny Tolentino

I can't say how long I battled to keep my sanity intact that night, because time had evaporated into space and become non-existent. I had heard my preacher dad talk about hell in the past, and I was sure I was now experiencing the depths of its horror. I desperately wanted out. No exit. The wicked, psychedelic images that flashed before my eyes would not release me. They just continued to mock my lame efforts to escape.

As the morning light appeared, I squinted at the blinding brightness. "Man, that was a really bad trip," I thought, testing the nightmare to make sure it was really over. It was not. But it was Thanksgiving, and I needed to pull myself together so I could meet the rest of my family at my grandmother's lake house.

I somehow managed to get my mind and body into my Chevy pickup and drive to the family gathering. I faked a smile as I greeted everyone, and then found a place to escape downstairs. From where I sat, I could see the lake, sleek as glass. Unlike me, it was calm. "You've got to get help," I thought.

"You're going insane," another voice shouted, "It's way too late."

I needed to do something quickly if I wanted to survive. With each second that passed, I felt as if the last ounce of sanity was being squeezed out of my brain. I wasn't sure what to do, so I decided that I had to tell my parents. It was my only hope. But how could I tell the two people I loved most that I had been using LSD? How could I be such a terrible disappointment to them? I had only played with drugs for fun, or so I thought. It wasn't like I was a rebellious kid trying to express some hidden anger towards some authority figure, or that I was looking for an escape from reality or something. I had been on my own since I was eighteen, and basically I was a fun-loving guy with a good job and a promising future. All the more reason that my parents would be shocked beyond comprehension. But my cheap form of entertainment had now gone wrong, and I saw no other way out but to tell them. They could help.

I found my way back to the crowded upstairs living room and approached my parents, who were talking with relatives. I tried not to attract attention and to remain emotionless when I asked them if they would come outside with me. They both immediately got up, worried looks on their faces, and followed me to my grandma's gravel driveway where I had parked my pickup. I lowered the tailgate and motioned for them to sit. They sat, silent and waiting. I was going to explain what was happening, but instead, I suddenly lost all control and screamed out, immediately unleashing the ravenous pack of fears that had been devouring my mind since last night.

"I'm going insane!" I yelled, "I'm losing my mind. I'll never be normal again." They stared at me in disbelief. "You've got to help me before it's too late. I don't want to go crazy. Please, pray for me! Help me, Mom, Dad, please, help me!" I pleaded, grabbing my Dad's arm, shaking with fear. I'm not sure my parents even realized what had happened to me. "I took some drugs. I'm so sorry," I explained, "and I'm losing my mind! Oh, Jesus, help me! Jesus, save me. Please, don't let me go insane. I'll give my life to You if You get me out of this. Please, Jesus, please," I begged.

I suddenly heard my dad's deep, heavily accented voice begin to pray, and I felt his large hand resting on my shoulder. So many times in the past, during the nine years that our family had lived on the mission field, I had listened to my dad pray, but his voice never sounded so good. I hung onto every word, desperate for a lifeline back to sanity.

When my dad finished praying, I instantly became aware that my senses and thought patterns were clear and organized. The tormenting fears were gone, as if they had never existed in the first place. It was like being let out of a dark cell and breathing fresh air again.

My mom and dad and I asked God to be merciful and keep me from suffering "flashbacks," as happens so many times with LSD. (And I am so thankful I never did.) We three left my grandmother's house with the excuse that I didn't feel well, and I stayed with my parents for a few days. They prayed with me and read the Bible to me and made sure I was okay before I returned home.

A Promise and a Second Chance

I believe that on that Thanksgiving Day, when I cried out for Jesus to spare my life and promised Him mine, that I was given a second chance. For sure I knew I would never mess around with LSD again. I had been freed from the most terrifying experience I had ever known, and for the first time in my life, I had my own encounter with God, and would never forget it.

Now, you would think that after an experience like this, I would have immediately joined some kind of church or something. But I didn't. I think deep in my heart, I was actually running from God. I thought He had a special reason for sparing my life, but I didn't want to be a preacher like my dad. I had seen what a sacrificial and difficult life he and my mom had lived when I was growing up in a third world country. It scared me to think that God might ask that of me, so I tried my best to ignore the "inner call" that I admit I heard. Instead, I filled my time with everything but the things I knew would bring me closer to God.

Hawaii

My job with a cable company took me to Hawaii where I spent all my free hours surfing and scuba diving, and loving it. I was only there for about six months when my mom got sick on a mission trip in Ecuador and nearly died in the intensive care unit of a small Ecuadorian hospital. My dad flew to Quito to bring her back home to the Carolinas as soon as she could travel. I flew home immediately to see her, but then within a week I had to return to Hawaii. But my mom was still sick. I didn't want to be so far away, so about a month later I got a new job and moved to Greensboro, North Carolina, and then later to Raleigh, much closer to home.

Meeting Owen and Wakeboarding

A buddy in Greensboro got me hanging out and shooting pool in my spare time ... and that's exactly where I was on the night that I would meet the man who would help me create a pivot point in my life. Bending over the pool table, cue stick in hand and seriously planning my next shot, I caught a glimpse out of the corner of my eye of a tall, blond guy approaching. He started up a conversation, and that was the beginning of a lasting friendship with Owen Parker.

It was Owen who first talked to me about "wakeboarding." I had never tried it before, but I was immediately interested. I had always loved water sports from the time I was a little kid and my grandfather used to let me drive his boat on the Great South Bay of Long Island. He made this board out of plywood and pulled me on it behind his twenty-foot wooden skiff. I can still remember the saltwater spray from the huge wake stinging my eyes as I struggled to stay balanced on two feet. Now Owen showed me this new, fancy fiberglass wakeboard that was named, "Evil Twin," and was describing a sport that sounded very much like my grandfather's idea of a good time. I was totally intrigued, and it wasn't too long after our first encounter at the pool hall that Owen took me out on the lake and I began to wakeboard for the first time.

Owen and I decided to move to Charlotte, North Carolina, where we started a business together. With our own company, we could make the money we needed and work the hours we wanted, and the rest of the time be out on the lake. It was a great plan! Our cable business did really well, and we had plenty of time to wakeboard. In the evenings, we would play pool or go to concerts and raves. Sometimes we would talk about God. Owen had grown up attending a Christian school, and so he and I both knew all the lingo, as well as the rules. We frequently made a conscious effort to follow those rules, but we always seemed to fall short.

I think "passion" would be a good word to describe my involvement in this new sport. I lived and breathed wakeboarding. Owen and I purchased all new equipment and a ski boat. We even rented a house in Tega Cay, South Carolina (a lakefront community) so we could be closer to the water. We spent every free minute on the lake. Within a short time, I was landing flips and trying new "tricks." I began to seriously think about competing, maybe even on the pro-tour level.

The Sport and the Gang Expand

While we lived in Tega Cay, I met two high school students, Mike and Andy, who were also addicted to wakeboarding. We all began to hang out together, and we all dreamed of becoming pro riders. We were totally dedicated to practicing long hours, even in the winter, wet suits and all, and I actually began to spend more time on the lake than I did on my job.

God Steps In

I believe it was during this time, when I was totally consumed with wakeboarding, that God started showing me little pictures of how I should serve Him. Not that He drew an actual picture, but thoughts would come to my mind frequently about a plan very different from my own. But I was a stubborn guy, busy and having fun, so I would turn my back, close my ears, and push Him away. Andy and I had been giving wakeboarding lessons to some doctors and some middle school students, and we would play with the idea of how cool it would be to have a camp so we could wakeboard all day long. We talked about it all the time, but it was only talk. I usually was quick to shove the suggestion to the side, knowing we couldn't let anything hinder our goal of traveling the pro circuit. A friend of mine who owns National RV Rentals offered to let us use an RV anytime we needed to get to a competition, and competing was definitely my goal.

It was when my little brother David came home for the summer after his first year of college and began to be a regular on the lake with us that I began thinking seriously about getting my life together. For sure it frustrated me to no end when he would get behind the boat and in no time be doing the tricks that it had taken me forever to learn! He was nine years younger than me, and it always seemed to me that there was nothing he couldn't do. Yet it wasn't his talent that got my attention that summer. It was his faith. He was totally unashamed of Jesus Christ. There was something about his relationship with God that was undeniable, real, and solid. He didn't talk about it much, and he didn't say anything about our "beer laden boats." He just challenged us to use our talents for Christ.

When David went back to school, I made an effort to attend church. At first I went sporadically. But this was the beginning of a meltdown of the walls I had built to keep God at a "safe" distance. In the past, Owen and I both had tried to live the way we knew was right. But somehow we just never quite made it. I was frustrated and empty. Maybe being at church once in a while would help.

The Breakthrough and Life Renewed

I was on a plane with Andy on the way back from the International Novice Tour Nationals, when I think I had a real " breakthrough" in my spiritual life. We had just competed in Texas, where the whole pro rider dream seemed possible. To qualify for that competition, I had become state champion in my division back home. I should have been really happy. But no. I was still struggling. I looked at who I was and who I wanted to be for God, and the gap was huge. So I made a simple, determined decision to change the things I was doing wrong. I would get out of some really bad relationships, break habits that were not bringing glory to God, and with God's help, become the kind of person that kids could look up to when they saw me on the winner's stand. I'm sure it was God who gave me the strength, because when I got back home, I stayed true to my decision. I started going to church regularly, attending both Sunday morning and evening services and Monday night prayer, as well as volunteering as a youth worker. Years ago, my parents had given me a Bible. It now went everywhere with me, so I could read whenever I got the chance.

For the very first time, I was actually having a relationship with Jesus Christ, and it was revolutionizing my life! After a while, Owen started attending church with me, and then we invited Mike and Andy. It was not unusual to see the whole wakeboard crew worshipping together. We began having Bible studies in our living room, and we often prayed together. Even our conversation was becoming more and more focused on God and His will.

The Accident That Changed Everything ... For the Better

Things were going well until one afternoon on the lake when my dreams of becoming a pro rider came crashing down as I felt my wakeboard pound the water and my knee totally give out as I landed the jump. I was not in a lot of pain, but immediately I knew I had done some major damage. A doctor later confirmed my suspicions. I was shocked. I just couldn't really believe I had torn my ACL! I had landed this flip with a twist perfectly so many times in the past. Why was this happening to me now? Now when everything seemed to be going so well? Now when I was riding better than ever? My pro wakeboarding dream was over.

DANNY TOLENTINO

I got a date for surgery, and hobbled out of the doctor's office using a borrowed pair of crutches. I couldn't believe it had happened. But here's the weird part. At the same time, I couldn't help but think that God was trying to get my attention. It was becoming obvious to me that His plan, not mine, was taking over. Wakeboarding couldn't be my passion; *He* would be. My dreams had to be His dreams.

Knee surgery went really well, and I worked hard at recovering fast. Unable to ride and by myself, I had a lot of time to think. I became convinced that I had been using my talents for the wrong purpose. I was finally ready to allow God to lead me into the ministry that I had been avoiding for a long time. And the great thing was that I was excited about it! As I lay there on the couch, my knee in a brace, everything that had been happening in my life for the past few years suddenly began to make total sense. God's "little pictures" became very clear to me, as if He had laid the map out on the coffee table and pointed the way. A brand new dream took the place of the pro circuit. There would be a camp for kids, clinics, and lessons. And it wouldn't just be limited to wakeboarding, but would include other core sports. The list went on and on. I knew now that the SouthTown Riders, as our group was named, had a much greater calling than to become pro riders. Instead of fame, our passion would become His compassion for youth everywhere who fight hard to find meaning in life. And so the true dream began. His.

Do not be surprised at the painful trial that you are suffering, as though something strange were happening to you. But rejoice because you now participate in the sufferings of Christ.

1 Peter 4:12,13

Suffering

Somehow we get this idea in our heads that nobody in the world has ever gone through the situations that we have gone through ... and are going through now. Unlikely. Being that there have only been billions of people on the planet, I'm pretty sure that one of those billions has had your experience.

There are two types of experiences for all humans: the good experiences and the bad experiences. Everybody has them. It's just that the bad ones can be so intense that it's impossible to focus outside ourselves long enough to observe anyone else, and our experience is too limited. We haven't compared notes. So we feel unique and alone. Sometimes we can get slammed with bad experience after bad experience until we get beaten down so much that there doesn't even seem like there is hope.

To make matters worse, there is this lie going around that once you become a Christian, your life becomes free of all bad things, and that if you are experiencing bad things, then you must be doing something wrong to make God mad, or have forgotten to ask forgiveness for a sin, and now you're paying the price—you're being somehow "punished." How are we supposed to be children of God and still be suffering? Well, it happens! Whether we like it or not, we still live in a world of pain and suffering. Even Jesus, the Son of God, had to deal with suffering and bad experiences. They aren't new and they're not going away.

The good news is that it's how we deal with the situation that gives us the ability to overcome our suffering.

Check this out, "Do not be surprised at the painful trial that you are suffering, as though something strange were happening to you. But rejoice because you now participate in the sufferings of Christ" (1 Peter 4:12,13).

Even Peter knew that life was going to be tough. Even after knowing Jesus! He even went to the extreme to say that you would now be singled out and suffer for being a Christian.

Although no suffering is good, self-inflicted suffering is the worst. People bring it on themselves with murder, slander, stealing, meddling, and other various things, which can all have painful consequences and result in suffering.

Where is the hope in knowing that you're going to suffer? It lies in this simple factor. Jesus. I have a friend whose sister tragically died unexpectedly; it was an out of the ordinary death. The following week, his best friend was racing his car and crashed and died instantly. Within a few months another friend and a roommate also were tragically killed. Yeah, I know it seems like he could blame God for all of this. He probably got very angry at God for letting this happen to him. But he didn't falter in putting his hope in God. Throughout the entire experience, he still trusted and found his joy in God. It was almost surreal. All that tragedy and still here's a guy who trusts God for his future and still has the ability to smile and laugh. He says this, "Jesus never backed away from me through all of this. I couldn't turn to my parents or friends. They were grieving as hard as I was. All I really had was Jesus. I continue to live for Him."

It's that ability to put our hope in Jesus that makes a believer in Jesus different from the rest of the world. It's almost not natural. When we give God praise and submit ourselves to Him through all sufferings, we become the greatest testimony of Hope. This life is temporary and so is the suffering in it. To praise God for all things shows others that we understand that He has truly saved us from eternal suffering and pain.

CORE ACTION

Think of the last time you suffered a great loss or disappointment. What was it?

How did you grow from the experience?

In what ways are you aware that God drew near to you?

What could you have done to rely more on God for comfort and understanding?

How can you use your experience to help someone else in a similar circumstance?

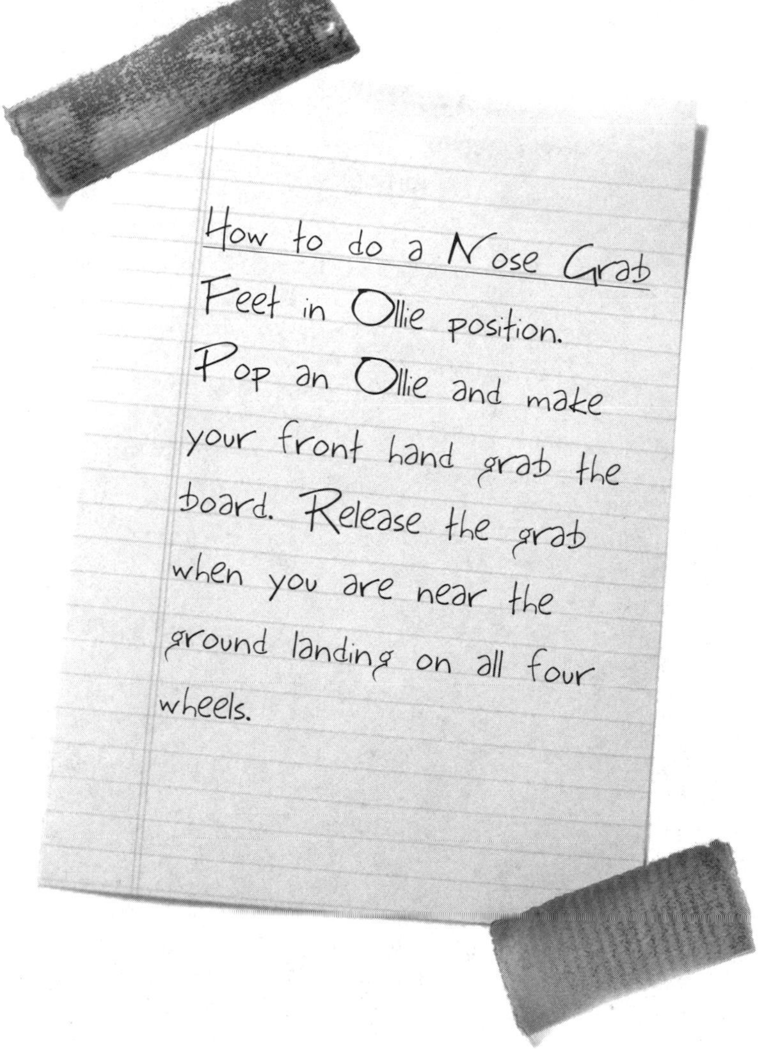

How to do a Nose Grab

Feet in Ollie position.
Pop an Ollie and make your front hand grab the board. Release the grab when you are near the ground landing on all four wheels.

Being a part of SouthTown has let me see the glory and love of God more clearly.

Chris DiMaggio, Age 12

**Even little lights make a
big difference.**

Light

One of my favorite places in the world is Lake Como in Italy. It's tightly tucked in and surrounded by the Alps. All the cities and villages are at lakeside, at the base of the mountains. Nighttime is spectacular, when you can see these intense clusters of sparkling lights reflected on the water.

There is one crazy vertical cliff with a single house at the top. I can't imagine the effort it took to build it and construct a road to get there. At night, when it's lit, no matter where you are down on the shores of the lake, you can see it for miles. But you can't see the streets that lead up to it. The path doesn't appear to be there. Just the house on the top. That light becomes the focal point for anyone who looks in that direction. But it doesn't matter that the path isn't apparent at first. As soon as you take the first step, you will find the path. The light on the top will lead you out of the valley, and guide you to the top of the mountain.
Imagine these same mountains in total darkness, without any lights at all, where you can't even see where sky meets the earth, it's so dark. Then someone in that house on the cliff turns on the light. It instantly separates light from darkness, heaven from earth.

Even little lights make a big difference.

Christ calls Himself "the Light of the world." He lights up things that we have never seen before. He brings the unknown into reality. The intangible, untouchable is suddenly known. No longer do we have to reach blindly to find our way around. "I am the light of the world. He who follows me shall not walk in darkness, but have the light of life" (John 8:12).

But then He turns around and calls *us* the light. "You are the light of the world …" (Matthew 5:14). What He means is that we reflect His light. Once He has illuminated truth and love for us, we are the keepers of the flame for Him. We are light, too. This is revelation light—why would we hide it? Jesus doesn't want greatness under a bowl. What happens when you put a candle under a jar? Eventually that light will fade and die out. Light has to be fed, fed by the exposure to the air, fed by the exposure to the darkness. Why would we put something so great into hiding? Into storage? He needs for His light to shine through us from the highest possible point, so that even those people in the valley can see Him, His good works, and His glory. If you lived in that house on the top of the mountain at Lake Como and wanted friends to visit you, how would they ever find your house in all that darkness if you didn't turn on the light? How will your friends ever come to Christ if you don't give them a light to see and follow?

"You are the light of the world. A city that is set on a hill cannot be hidden. Nor do they light a lamp and put it under a basket, but on a lampstand and it gives light to all who are in the house. Let your light so shine before men, that they may see your good works and glorify your Father in heaven" (Matthew 5:14-16).

Build your city on the hill so people can see you. Among all the others, be a luminary. Don't be an ordinary Christian. Shine!

CORE ACTION

Get a flashlight. Stand in the middle of your room at night. Turn all the lights off. Notice the darkness and how uncomfortable it is, even though you know where you are and know where everything is. There's nothing to fear, and yet you are uneasy. Notice that you blend into shadows and darkness.

Now shine the flashlight on you. Notice that in the darkness, the smallest light makes the biggest difference. Now, if someone else were to come into your room, he would easily see you. Notice that as the light reflects off you, it illuminates other things in the room. This is like the light of Christ. It shines on you and in you. In the darkness, you stand in light where you are easily seen by other people who are searching.

Now that you know that the light of Christ makes it easy for people to see you, what are they seeing?

OWEN'S STORY

In 1997 I was celebrating my twentieth birthday in much the same way that I did my nineteenth. I was drinking underage in a bar just a few miles from my home in Durham, North Carolina. The bartenders all knew me, and I had long ago convinced them that I was twenty-one, so I never needed a fake ID. There really wasn't anything special about this day; I drank on a pretty regular basis. However, being thrown in jail for DUI and underage drinking did change my daily routine just a little bit. I was never the type to learn things easily, so within months of being bailed out of jail by my parents, I was back at it again, only this time my choice of bars was significantly limited since the word was out about my age. Have you ever looked back on your life and realized that a certain mement that seemed innocent enough really turns out to be a major turning point? Well, I was about to have one of those moments.

I walked into one of the only places that still hadn't figured out my age, and I proceeded to have my usual. By usual I mean whatever beer was on special. Halfway through a really bad game of pool, I overheard a short, dark-skinned punk talking about surfing in

> **He has brought me this far, and His word promises that He will never leave me nor forsake me.**
>
> **Owen Parker**

Hawaii. I had seen him walk in earlier, and decided that I would probably try and fight him later on that night if nothing better came along, but since I had just come back from surfing off of the North Carolina coast, I changed my mind and went over to talk to him. However, I didn't completely rule out the possibility of a fight. I figured I would just play it by ear. I was really interested in hearing about actual big wave surfing, since surfing in North Carolina usually just means you have a seven-foot longboard on a four-foot, shore breaking wave. He introduced himself as Danny Tolentino, and we proceeded to start a long conversation about surfing, which we later finished while smoking a rather large joint. Did I fail to mention that we had a lot of things in common? Besides, all I really cared about at the time was beer, drugs, and women ... and that order changed periodically depending on the availability of any of those items.

I hate to drag Danny's secrets into the open, but like I said, we had a lot in common. Danny had a job, so his priorities were slightly more focused than mine, but not by much. That was pretty much the life-changing moment. Doesn't sound like much, does it? Well, if I speed up the story a little bit, this will come to make sense.

Because of our common interests, and the fact that I really wanted to get out on my own, I moved into Danny's apartment after only about two months. It also didn't hurt matters that he could buy beer anywhere, and we could split the hassle of driving home drunk. This was the perfect opportunity for me. If anyone reading this has ever gone back to live with your parents after being away at school, you know what I mean. Moving on.

After a while, I became acutely aware that Danny was making a great deal more money than I thought I would ever make coming out of college, and Danny had never spent one day in college. Come to think of it, I wasn't quite sure how much he paid attention in high school either. I didn't really feel like going back to school, so I began to pester Danny about getting a job with him, and he informed me that he was thinking about quitting his current job and going to work for himself. He offered to bring me in if I could help him come up with the cash he needed to get started. So, I went to my parents, did a little sweet-talking, and we were in business. Picture this: You are twenty years old, own your own business, and make enough money to close down every bar and strip club on the east coast. Does that sound good to anyone else? Well, it shouldn't. But it sure did to me at the time! Things weren't always easy, and the money didn't always flow like wine, but you get the gist of it.

Danny and I Are in Business

Danny and I based our company in Charlotte, North Carolina, and that is where we lived for the next few years. Things really didn't change much between 1997 and 2000. We worked hard; we played really hard; and we spent money like Donald Trump. We never got a chance to go surfing, but that wasn't a problem thanks to a little device I bought the summer before Danny and I met. It was my first wakeboard. Obrien's "Evil Twin" to be exact, complete with sandlestrap bindings, super stretch slalom ski rope, and a life jacket that looked more suited for a bassmasters tournament. Danny had never really seen a wakeboard in person before, and to be honest, this really wasn't much of a wakeboard. But, it was all we had. Did I mention that the life jacket perfectly matched our Ranger bass boat that was frequently our towboat of choice? Well, this brings us to another good skipping point. Wakeboarding pretty much occupied every free daylight hour that we had for the next year or so, and our nightlife didn't change much at all. It may have actually gotten a little worse, since I could afford a lot more drugs than I was used to.

An Eight Month Break: Move to Virginia

I think it was in 1999 that Danny and I dissolved the company for a number of different reasons. I moved to Virginia for a while, and we both went to work for other companies. We stayed in touch fairly frequently, and we often discussed the possibility of me moving back to Charlotte and renting a house on the lake together. During this time I started to notice things about Danny that were changing. For instance, when I would call him to brag about my girls or my drugs, or my girls with drugs, he wouldn't sound quite as interested as he used to. In fact, on several occasions he asked me if all of that really made me happy. At the time, my answer was always an emphatic, Yes! It's hard to say that you

I could tell you almost anything there was to know about religion and God, but none of it meant a thing to me.

don't want all the things that your body craves, isn't it? I mean, I was having way too much fun.

Return to Charlotte

Well, after about eight months, I moved back to Charlotte and lived with different friends until Danny and I could find a house together. Now comes the part that won't make a lot of sense without a bit of a flashback, and I don't mean the drug related kind. So here we go. I attended a private Christian school for the first eighteen years of my life. I could tell you almost anything there was to know about religion and God, but none of it meant a thing to me. There you have it, flashback finished. My high school career in a nutshell.

Getting back to the story, Danny and I started working for the same company in Charlotte, and we found our house on the lake. We took on a

few roommates, and our days were rarely any different from this: wake up at 7:30, work until 1:30, get on the water and ride until dark, then get ready to do it all over again tomorrow. It was perfect. Except, did you notice that there wasn't any bar time in there anymore? Yeah, so did I.

Eventually I started making a little more time for my old illegal hobbies, not to mention old friends. I continued to notice things that were different about Danny and some of my revolving roommates, but I couldn't quite put my finger on it. For instance, the beer and friends that I frequently brought to the house seemed to bother Danny a little. He didn't really get mad at me about it, but he was obviously upset that I was doing it. This bothered me a little; after all, I was twenty-one now. The same guy that I used to party with was now making me feel guilty about partying, and he wasn't even trying.

It took a while for me to get up the nerve, but I finally confronted my roommates. Or maybe it was the other way around. Anyway, I was informed that they were all Christians, and they didn't want me drinking in the house. They didn't care what I did outside the house, but they were afraid that their friends and family would associate my party trash with them. Nice time for a news flash. I didn't take it very well. This completely blew my mind. Actually, I was a little bit mad about it. Who

Tantrum

Come in with a progressive cut. When you get to the bottom of the wake, drop your back hand and square up to the wake. You should really wait for a good pop off the wake before you throw this trick. Throw yourself back as if you are doing a back flip on a trampoline or into a swimming pool. Make sure to throw your head straight back and spot the second wake. Once you see the second wake, start spotting your landing and hold onto the handle tight. Ride away clean!

knew more about this stuff than me? Remember the flashback? I had countless hours of Bible class under my belt. I mean, I was a Christian too, wasn't I? I had the right to do whatever I wanted! So I did; just outside the house. I wasn't going to let them guilt trip me! I was a Christian! At least, I'm pretty sure I was. So I told them how I felt. I told them that God and I had made an agreement a long time ago. I believed in Him, and He just let me do my thing. Besides, saying that you believe in Jesus is all it takes, right? I had done that plenty of times. So that was that. I put them in their place, and I went back to my daily routine. Except that I did tone down on the extra curricular activities just to avoid confrontation. I even started helping out some with this new ministry thing they were trying to get going called SouthTown Riders.

Life Takes Another Turn

Well, that should be the end of it. I had it all figured out, right? My life made sense. I had everything that a guy my age could want. I had a well paying job; I came and went as I pleased; I had plenty of female companionship. So why did I start to feel so distant from everybody? Why did I feel so alone even when I was surrounded by friends? Why did my life that I thought made so much sense seem so empty and meaningless? I couldn't figure it out. I was a good person. I had almost stopped drinking; I did quit drugs; I even quit smoking. What was my problem?

Months went by with me asking those same questions over and over again. I would lie in bed with my girlfriend at night and wonder why I felt so empty. Eventually I remembered something that my teachers used to talk about all the time. Prayer. That was it! I had forgotten that Christians were supposed to pray. So I sat up in bed and I prayed to God to make my life better, then I curled up right back next to my girlfriend. I was confident that I had figured it out; all I had to do was wait. So I waited. I had a few beers, slept with my girlfriend, and waited. More months went by and I still saw nothing. So I prayed again. This time I confronted God about His slow response time, and asked Him what the hold up was. Here comes another one of those life changing moments. Only this one wasn't any fun at all. The very next day I began to see things in a slightly different perspective. I began to feel guilty about things that I had never felt guilty about in my life. I felt awful after I stayed with my girlfriend for a night. I felt like I was looked down upon every time I cursed at someone or drank too much. I even felt guilty about calling myself a Christian. Pretty much everything I did was making me feel worse about myself. This was not what I had asked God for.

I had asked Him why He had not responded to me. BINGO! The light went on like a flash of lightning. God *was* responding. Only, He wasn't telling me what I wanted to hear! He was telling me that all the things in my life that I craved were keeping Him from coming closer to me. I knew it! That was why I never really trusted Him when I was younger, because I knew he would just take away all the things that I wanted. I just knew that he would take every fun thing away from me.

Now I had a real dilemma. I now knew what was causing my heart to break, but I wasn't sure I wanted it fixed. I wasn't sure I wanted to give up my girlfriend and my good job and my free time to ski. That was like asking me to give up my entire life! Have you ever had that kind of decision to make? Well, I didn't want it! So I decided to ignore it. I would pretend like it never happened. That would be my solution. It should work, right? Ignoring the problem will just make it go away right? Wrong! The guilt remained. The self-doubt, the depression, the complete lack of joy! They stayed with me.

Now I was in a worse dilemma. What do you do in a situation like that? I wasn't sure how to get out of this mess. I was perfectly happy just months before, and now I couldn't get back there. So I went to the person who got me in it in the first place. God. I got on my knees and I told God that I was through with the pain. I didn't want it anymore, and I was willing to sacrifice just a few things to get rid of the heartache. I even told Him I would give up wakeboarding and drinking, and I did! I felt a little bit better, but I still could tell there was something wrong. I could still feel a searing pain deep in my heart. So, I went to the one place that I knew I could find someone with answers. Church.

Now Church

I had been to church a thousand times before, but this time was different. This time I actually wanted to be there. This time I had a purpose for being there. I listened to the pastor preach about forgiveness, and I cried through most of the service. I waited till it was over, including the altar call, and I went and found Danny's father who also happened to be an elder in the church. I explained my situation to him and I asked if he could help me feel better. His answer surprised me. He said, No! But he said he did know someone who could. He then called over another elder who looked like a linebacker for the Packers, and I thought to myself, "Here comes the pain!" If this giant put his hands on me and started screaming for demons to come out, I was going to hit the door in a hurry. Was this the guy who was supposed to help me? Again the answer was, No. They explained to me that I needed to be saved. Oh, gee, what a revelation, I already knew that part. In fact I told them I already was saved. I spoke the name of Jesus a dozen times when I was in high school. I was beginning to think

this was just another run around until Danny's dad showed me the second half of a Scripture that I had long forgotten. See, not only do you have to confess with your mouth, you have to believe in your heart that Jesus is Lord. There was the key word, "believe." This would be the first time that I had ever actually believed the words that I was about to speak.

These two men proceeded to lead me through a prayer that had me confessing my sins out loud, and asking a living man named Jesus to forgive me of them and to dwell inside my heart. When I was in high school, I had said all of this before, minus a few sins I had yet to commit. However, there was something different about this particular time. I felt a weight lifting off my spirit, and a warmth and love filling my soul, and I knew that from that day forward I would never be the same again. Did a light flash in front of me? No. Did a choir sing hallelujah? Not exactly. Did a halo appear above my head? Absolutely not. Did I walk out of that church a perfect and holy Christian? No. But what did happen was this: From that day forward I no longer felt condemned for the things I had done in the past, and I knew I had help steering clear of them in the future. It was absolutely a life changing experience, but it didn't happen overnight.

My life is still changing today, and it will continue to do so until the day that I die. Am I perfect? No. But I also know now that I don't have to be. Jesus took care of that. At this point, I would like to invite anyone who can relate to any part of my story to seek out a Christian friend or a pastor and tell them how you feel. You can even contact me or someone else at www.southtownriders.com. Believe me, we personally can't help you, but we know someone who can!

Today

Well, that just about brings us to the present. Do you remember all the things I said I was afraid of losing? I lost that fear, along with most of those things. But I didn't lose everything, in fact, I found out that there were quite a few things that God wanted me to keep, and a few that He wanted me to have that I had never even dreamed of. The things I say that I lost were not actually lost. I willingly gave them up because I didn't want them anymore, and in return, God gave me other things that far surpassed my expectations. I still get to wakeboard all the time, but now I get more joy out of it because I do it with SouthTown and God uses it for His glory. I have a wife who is involved with the STR ministry, and she is far greater than any girlfriend I ever had, and I don't say that just because she is a Christian. I was given the opportunity to be the lead singer of SouthTown's band and use a vocal talent that I never knew I had until God revealed its purpose. I have also been given several other opportunities to use my God given talents on national television for both SouthTown and other ministries.

OWEN PARKER

Years ago I met a punk kid that liked to surf. Who would have thought that God had so much planned for us in the future? I hope God keeps me involved with STR, but I know that no matter what, He has great plans in store for me as long as I let Him lead the way. God brought me all the way from a bar in Durham to a ministry in Charlotte that reaches thousands of people with the gospel of Jesus Christ. He has brought me this far, and His word promises that He will never leave me nor forsake me.

Commit everything you do to the Lord.
Trust Him to help you do it and He will (Psalm 37:5).

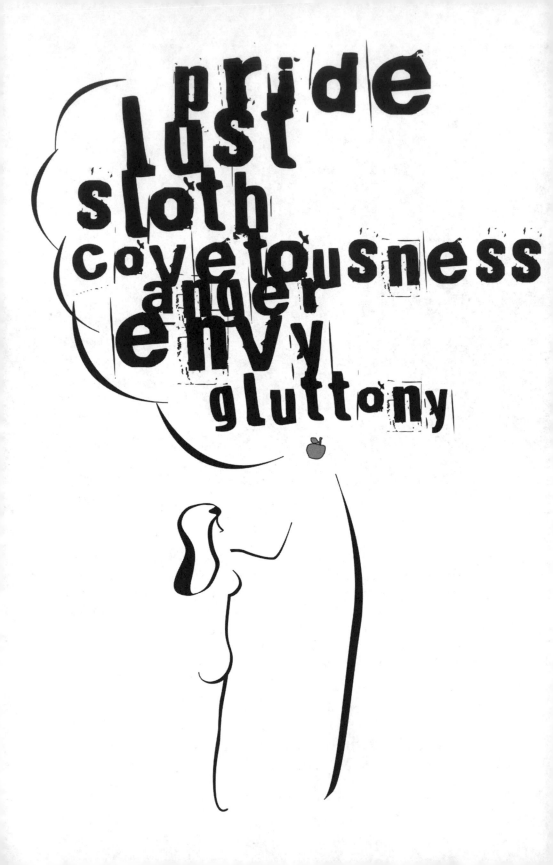

The Seven Deadly Sins

"SIN" seems to be an awkward word for us to use today.
When we describe things that are wrong, we're much more
comfortable with, "He committed a CRIME," or "That was BAD," or
"I was WRONG." But the truth of the matter is that all wrong things
ARE sin. While the Bible is clear that sin is breaking the Laws and
heart of God, we humans like to grade sin ... as though one sin
could be less wrong than another. Hey, we all agree that murder is a
huge sin. But what about little white lies? They're small sins with
good intentions. So they're not so bad, right? Don't be so sure. Sin is
sin is sin. If you've told a little white lie, you've lied. If you've taken a
paperclip from class without asking, you've stolen. If you've
worshipped a famous athlete or a rock star, you're guilty of the sin of
idolatry. The list of our failures is endless. That's the bad news. The
good news is that we're forgiven.

God laid down His Law in the Ten Commandments. Anything you do
that breaks one of the Commandments is sin.

It couldn't be more simple and straightforward. God has laid it all
out. But it's human nature to try to define the distinctions between
right and wrong. Trying to grade sin from "Serious Offense" to
"Nearly Innocent Mistake" is as old as time. Long ago and over many
centuries, theologians drew up a list of offenses that described the
evil nature of human beings. They were ranked in order by how
much they went against love, from the least offensive to the most.
The worse the sin, the more you could be sure that the sinner was
thinking only of himself. They are called The Seven Deadly Sins. You
won't find them in the Bible. Humans thought them up. But they are
famous, and they are one more way to look at how flawed we are.

Although they do not define all sin, they are interesting to study.

1. LUST

Being sexually attracted to someone you shouldn't be attracted to

2. GLUTTONY

Taking more than your share, or eating too much

3. GREED

Unnatural need to get and keep money or material possessions

4. SLOTH

Lazy, and always taking the easy way out

5. ANGER

Free-floating rage at everything and everyone, bad temper

6. ENVY

Wanting what other people have and thinking you deserve it more

7. PRIDE

Taking credit when things go right, even though you know God did it

DEALING WITH LUST

Picture in your mind a ferocious bulldog tied to his doghouse with a strong metal chain. His owner tosses him a juicy piece of steak, but it falls outside his reach. With mouth slobbering, he uses all his weight and pulls against his chain, dragging his doghouse until he can snatch the steak and gobble it down. Lust is much like this scene. You see something or someone that you feel you must have, some pleasure you must fulfill. It's outside the confines of what you know to be right, but its strong attraction and your hunger for it consume you until you struggle against everything you know to be true and right to get it. You may even try to justify your actions—"dragging your beliefs behind you."

Jesus talks very openly about sexual lust in His famous Sermon on the Mount.

"You have heard that it was said to those of old, 'You shall not commit adultery.' But I say to you that whoever looks at a woman to lust for her has already committed adultery with her in his heart" (Matthew 5:28).

The known penalty for adultery in the time of Christ was stoning to death. Jesus equated even looking at a woman with wrong intentions as being punishable by death. That's a pretty heavy consequence. His message clearly warned that you can lust with your mind, even if you don't follow through with physical actions, and both are just as sinful.

The Bible tells us to "flee youthful lusts" (2 Timothy 2:22), "abstain from fleshly lusts" (1 Peter 2:11), "make no provision for the flesh, to fulfill its lusts" (Romans 13:14).

These seem like hard requirements, especially when you are bombarded with sexually enticing temptations from all angles in our world. Satan throws you the "meat" through TV, Internet, advertising, clothing styles, and every other avenue he can find to seduce your

Flee also youthful lusts; but pursue righteousness, faith, love, peace, with those who call on the Lord out of a pure heart

(2 Timothy 2:22).

I can do all things through Christ who strengthens me

(Philippians 3:4).

mind. Yet the Lord himself commands us to keep our eyes from wandering and our minds pure. He knows the dangers that hide behind lust: sex addiction, pornography, guilt, loss of self worth, inability to have a healthy relationship with the opposite sex, confusion with real love, and the list goes on and on.

Lust is not just confined to sex. Anything that you "drool at the mouth for" and entices you to compromise your walk with God becomes lust. He alone should be desired with such intensity. That's the bottom line. Anything else that takes His place in our lives, i.e., lust for money, fame, etc. causes us to commit adultery in our relationship with Him.

The great part about having a relationship with Christ is that He helps you to stay close and clean. He gives us guidelines to follow. He then gives us the strength to obey. He just needs a willing heart and mind.

"Flee also youthful lusts; but pursue righteousness, faith, love, peace, with those who call on the Lord out of a pure heart" (2 Timothy 2:22).

"I can do all things through Christ who strengthens me" (Philippians 3:4).

CORE ACTION

When you are contemplating an action that could involve lust, check this list before you act:

1. Would I do this if I knew someone was watching?
Yes   No

2. Would I do this if I knew that someone would find out later?
Yes   No

3. Do I have a sense that this is wrong?
Yes   No

4. Are there negative consequences to this action?
Yes   No

5. If I do this will it break God's heart?
Yes   No

If you answered "no" to 1, or 2, and "yes" to 3, 4, or 5, then make a conscious decision NOT to engage in the particular action, and ask God to give you the strength to carry out your decision.

DEALING WITH GLUTTONY

The dictionary describes gluttony as "habitual greed or excess in eating." The Bible clearly defines it as "sin," and tags it alongside drunkenness every time it's mentioned. There is a law in Deuteronomy 21:20-21 that punishes gluttony (along with drunkenness and disobedience to parents) by stoning to death! Now that's a pretty heavy penalty for a little rebellion, partying, and pigging out! But gluttony, along with her biblical twin, drunkenness, is certainly part of a bigger issue of self-control and moderation.

It's human nature to pick and choose our favorite sins. Most of us are very clear about sins that are obviously wrong ... like murder. We tend to ignore the ones we don't think are so bad ... like gluttony. And yet, nowhere in the Bible are sins "ranked" so that we can pick and choose. God commands; He doesn't suggest.

I tackle this issue with care and vigor. I've found this to be a very touchy subject among friends and family. It seems that we're taught to justify the things we do that bring us pleasure or freedom from stress. On the other hand, restraint and moderation can be pretty tough. Let's take alcohol, for instance. Alcohol in proper moderation doesn't force us into drunkenness. But in the United States, unlike many of the world's cultures, we rarely promote the use in moderation. Sure, we see the alcohol ads on TV with their tag lines, "Drink Responsibly," but this is just a required disclaimer. And who knows what this really means, anyway? The irony is that drinking—even a small drink—can instantly, automatically make you less responsible. Even one drink can lower your inhibitions and erode your judgment. And when your judgment is gone, frankly your decisions are ... well ... stupid.

We know that drinking too much is bad because the direct result is drunkenness. The Bible tells us that at the point of being drunk, drinking moves into the realm of sin. Romans 13:13 clearly says: "Let us walk **properly,** as in the day, not in revelry and **drunkenness** ..."

There are a thousand reasons not to drink, not the least of which is that it's illegal for youth. In most states, the legal drinking age is 21. Get caught; get arrested. And of course, it messes up your head so that you do things you deeply regret in the morning. It's also addictive, and can ruin your life, relationships, career, and health in a shorter period of time than you might imagine. In worst-case scenarios, it can kill you in one night. At SouthTown we have to deal with people partying and getting drunk all the time. In fact, it's one of the most common subjects of Christian plays for youth groups … for good reason.

But gluttony isn't only about alcohol. It's also about eating too much. (Remember that in the Bible gluttony is always mentioned alongside drunkenness). Like alcohol, food gets advertised all the time on TV. There are no disclaimers at the ends of the ads that say, "Eat responsibly."

Now here's where it gets hard. While it's easy to walk away from alcohol completely and forever, you can't do that with food. You HAVE to eat. So developing habits of healthy choice and moderation are a little harder. And worse, in our culture, we have food that's been developed for entertainment. It has no nutritional value; it just tastes great and it's fun to eat. Like cookies and chips and candy bars. You know. We call it "junk food" for good reason. It's worthless junk. And we love it. We want it. We've got to have it. Lots of it.

And even healthy food is pushed at us. We are told, "Clean your plate!" At least with alcohol, excess will eventually render a drinker unconscious. With eating, excess can go way too far with no consequences except maybe having to wait a little while for things to settle before you dive into another bag of chips. It's really easy to eat too much.

I am the living bread which came down from heaven. If anyone eats of this bread, he will live forever…

(John 6:51).

When eating goes wrong, you ignore your body's warning signs of "feeling full," and you eat beyond your need. Now you're not going to die that night or get into a car accident because you were impaired by your cheeseburger, but you will slowly gain weight. Over time you will find yourself getting heavier and heavier. It is not an instantaneous death. You simply slow down, become less active, and increase chances for a lot of illnesses and disabilities as you grow older and wider. Both sins, gluttony and drunkenness, lead to death … and a miserable life up until that point.

Gluttony is selfish. It's the ME. Because our stomachs are the easiest things to satisfy, we might comfort ourselves by indulging when we are sad, bored, or depressed. There doesn't *seem* to be anything wrong with that. Yet filling emptiness in ourselves with food means that we don't trust God with our happiness. In a sense, food becomes our god when we turn to it to meet our needs … other than that of nourishing our bodies.

The truth is that only true satisfaction and happiness in life come from Christ. He alone can fill us with all we need.

CORE ACTION

Keep track of how many times you get something to eat during the day. Keep a one-day food diary on a typical day. (Snacks and "just taking a taste" count!)

When you went for food, were you always hungry? Yes/No

If not, why did you eat?

What other need might you be fulfilling by eating?

Learn to leave food on your plate if you have been served an "unhealthy" portion (bigger than you think reasonable). Count how many times in a week you ate everything because you felt guilty or thought it would be rude not to "clean your plate."

Make a list of the times you ate this week until you were full and then "ate some more," for no apparent reason. Now, give serious thought to the reason that wasn't apparent. Why did you do it?

How many "empty foods" did you eat (chips, cookies, candy bars, etc.) this week? Keep a journal.

Monday

Tuesday

Wednesday

Thursday

Friday

Saturday

Sunday

Remind yourself that excess
eating is sin, and ask God to
help you develop self-control
and moderation in your eating
habits.

Remind yourself that drinking
isn't legal for you now, and
ask God to keep you safe
from temptation and to
protect your friends who
drink when their judgment is
impaired. Ask God to free
them from this sin and keep
them safe from temptation.

**The team members
all talk about simple
things and express their
daily walk with God,
which lets me do the
same in a cool way.**
Kristin Mayhall Age 15

DEALING WITH GREED

Greed is when you have enough, and want too much more—especially those things you can't or shouldn't have. It's a sin.

The story of Adam and Eve has always caught me off guard for some reason. Theirs is the ultimate story of greed and sin. You have two people who had just been created. Not just being born from a mother but being physically created by God as grown individuals. Then these two are given the most ideal plot of real estate on the planet to live in: The Garden of Eden. Nice trees, plenty of food, no hard labor, furry woodland creatures, the ultimate vacation getaway without the hefty price tag.

Adam's responsibility was the creative job of naming all of the Creations that God had conceived. He and Eve were simply caretakers of the garden; they never had to work for their food. Then the big bonus: They had the chance to walk in the garden with God. What more do you need? That is the burning question for all of humanity, because it seems that the nature of man is to always need something more than what he/she has right now. All that wonder and glory Adam and Eve had ... and they *had* to go and covet the one thing they weren't supposed to have. Of course, it would be the tree of the knowledge of good and evil—it was the one thing God told them not to even touch. It wasn't a simple fruit with fruit they wanted to taste, it was the power this tree possessed. This tree was to make them like God, giving them the power to become like Him, letting them see the difference between good and evil.

They both wanted this, but it was the only thing they couldn't have. They listened to the truthful deceit and acted upon their desires. The result of their actions and disobedience was the banishment from bliss and their walks with God. Now life would be hard work and toil for food and shelter.

What does this mean for us? Well, now we have to deal with the fallen nature of man: the ability to commit sin. This is in every human. We're now bound to the knowledge of good and evil, and the result for us is death.

Back then, the only way for humans to get back into right standing with God was through sacrifice and law ... hence the Old Testament practice of blood sacrifices for forgiveness of offenses to God and the writing of the law to define those offenses that humans now had knowledge of. The people were still bound to the knowledge of good and evil.

Then Jesus makes His appearance on the earth. The whole nature that Adam had left behind is getting ready to be broken. It's through Jesus' death and resurrection that He corrects the wrongs of Adam and now ushers in a new phase of life for humankind. It's called "being born again." Not the physical rebirth, going back into your mother's womb and being birthed, but a spiritual rebirth.

What is included in spiritual rebirth? The most important of them all, we are no longer bound to sin. The bonds of the tree of the knowledge of good and evil have been broken, and man has been brought back into proper communion with God again.

What does it mean for the born again believer? Law is what bound man to sin, for without the Law, man wouldn't know sin. Without sin there would be no law. No need! With Jesus' ultimate atonement, He put man back into position to defeat sin. The position to defeat the law with Grace is given to us by Jesus in Romans 6:14. This brings us to the position of being free in Christ. Here. Read for yourself:

" For sin shall not have dominion over you: for you are not under the law, but under grace" (Romans 6:14).

It's easy for us to define things in life as sin. And sometime we bind ourselves to the fear of sin, so we create laws or rules out of fear of committing those sins. But if we lived outside the reach of the tree of the knowledge of good and evil, we would live in full freedom of Christ. It's the power to not sin, not because of laws, but because of the destruction of the power of the sin by Jesus. It's the power to destroy the original want to eat from the tree of the knowledge of good and evil, and return to the way things were—communion with God. Jesus had that communion; He paid the ultimate sacrifice so we could also have it. Every human longs for that communion. The only way to that communion is through Christ. It all started with man wanting to be more like God, and now ends with man wanting to be more like Jesus.

CORE ACTION

It's time to take inventory of your belongings. Be totally honest. We're not going to ask you to give anything away, but we want you to challenge yourself and ask some hard questions:

What thing do you own that you value beyond all other things? What would you do if something happened to it? If you think you couldn't survive losing it, figure out how it fills such an important place in your life. Are you trusting it for your security and happiness instead of trusting God?

What do you have too much of, and yet still you want more? What if you take so much of something that other people don't get any? Like potato chips in a bowl. How does it make you feel to know that your greed has made other people unhappy or kept them from getting something they need or want? Is this of God?

Now here's the hard part. Take something you value and share it with someone. You don't necessarily have to give it away, but you have to stop hoarding it and keeping it from being enjoyed by someone with whom you could share it. For example, let someone ride your skateboard for a little while. Notice how it feels to let someone experience your board and know that you made that happen by not being greedy. Feels good, doesn't it? God is pleased.

DEALING WITH SLOTH

Sloth is about being lazy. And being lazy is about being fearful. To conquer sloth, you conquer fear. You go big.

At SouthTown Riders, we have plenty of video footage of falls. Some are spectacular; some are funny; some are heart-stopping; all are about learning. We have people who approach sports carefully, too carefully. They're afraid to fall. But guess what? You *have* to learn to fall ... and learn to land. Falling gives you motivation to not fall and confidence that if you do fall, you'll get back up. You'll never learn to do a trick if you won't fall. When you go, go big and fall big.

When you don't fall, it tells you there's a problem—you're comfortable ... and edging toward "lazy." And if you're comfortable, it means that you're not trying hard enough. Go bigger! Even when you think you've topped it, there's always more. Reaching is never over.

Your idea of "big" is relative to your ideas and ability. God wants us to be big and make the ultimate—not just a Wake Jump or just an Ollie. He wants us to fly, to fly high ... and look good doing it. Take it over the top. Do it even more. Why stop at Level One? Why not create the next level?

In wakeboarding or skateboarding or snowboarding or BMX cycling, you're either going to fall or you're not. God doesn't give us the spirit of fear. He teaches that all things are possible through Him. Why wouldn't you try to go big? Paul wrote from his prison cell, "I can do everything through him who gives me strength" (Philippians 4:13).

Fear is a mental game we play with ourselves. Fear is ingrained in us, and refined from an early age to preserve us from harm. When you fell and hurt your knee, your mom ran to you with a Band-Aid. She taught you to recognize consequences. She taught you to fear. And while healthy fear is good (it can keep you from doing something that will get you seriously hurt or killed), it can also overwhelm your courage when it shouldn't. It stops you from trying. You can't let that happen.

When I have a fear of trying a BIG trick, I know I'll fall. It's part of learning. I ask God to guide me, protect me, and give me strength. Then I don't think. I just do. If I fall, I fall. But if I jump the wake, I fly.

be only 10 inches. It doesn't matter. Even the 10-footer will want more.

After you've nailed a big trick or mastered a tough skill, pass on the ability to go big. Encourage everyone who's interested to follow you. Call everyone to win. Pass on trick tips. Instead of being proud, appreciate the differences. Think to yourself, "I was once there. Follow me!" This is the concept of a good shepherd. If less skilled people see you do it, they'll feel more confident. They'll be able to close the fear once they see that the consequences aren't so serious. Maybe that's the way you learned, too.

God is greater than you are. You can be greater than you think. Nothing is impossible when God is with you. The only thing holding you back is you.

Definition of bravery is to do something you're really afraid of. Be brave. Go Big or Go Home.

Of course, you build foundations for each trick. Jesus can give skill to you in pieces. You work your way up trick by trick. You can't skip steps. For example, you can't land a big wakeboard trick if you can't swim and have never seen a boat before. You have to put some things into place first.

Whether you land your big trick or don't, God sees your effort beyond all anxiety, fear, and suffering. God is pleased with you. It doesn't matter what anyone else says. We serve God, not our friends. And the definition of "big trick" is relative. One person's big trick is maybe 10 feet; another's may

CORE ACTION

Wait until dark and keep the lights off. Walk into a room you're not in very often. Don't walk slowly. Walk fast. You'll probably be super scared. You might even stumble into something. Now back out to the doorway and turn the light on. Examine the room carefully. Turn the light back off. Repeat. Walk fast into the room.

Notice the difference in how you feel between the first time and the second time. The second time in, you're more relaxed because now you know where things are. First you bumped into them. Then you saw them. You have experience. That walk in the dark is easier now. Visually pace through the "dangers." Pick a different route into the room, and notice that you're still okay. Pray, "Lord, let me experience everything along the way."

Hold your hands out in total darkness. Fear heightens your senses. Use that. Reach out. You can't see it, but you go for it anyway. You know it's there.

You now have a peace about navigating. Your experience will take you easily to the new places in the room. Faith surpasses your ability. Like life. Like going big.

Christians are cool, and God will come through!

Gage Thompson, Age 15

DEALING WITH ANGER

Anger means that you're outraged and enraged, and there's no forgiveness in you. You've been wronged and forgiveness has not replaced all the rage.

I really believe that anger starts in families. The nuclear family—mom, dad, and kids—is no more. We're now "Salad Families"—people just tossed in a bowl together. Free-floating anger starts when we're kids in pain, wanting a parent's love … and it's not there.

But parental love is the role of Jesus. He's the perfect Father who loves, listens, hears, and answers our prayers in His time. (I remind you to be patient in "His time," because even if the answer to your prayer comes later than you expect, the surprise is a lot better.)

Get anger under control. Your emotions are yours alone. You can control them. Do it.

The ultimate debt has already been paid for you, leaving for you the ultimate freedom. So every offense against you doesn't have to eat you alive. Most offenses are pretty small. You have to forgive people who offend and hurt you, no matter how bad they are. The Bible instructs us to do it quickly before the offense against you eats at you and does you damage—not from the offender, but from yourself!

"Be angry, but do not sin; do not let the sun go down on your anger" (Ephesians 4:26).

We learn the practice and principles of forgiveness from God. God didn't have to forgive us. He could have dwelled on our transgressions. But He could see beyond circumstances, and put our offenses behind Him. Do you remember the story of Noah? God was fed up with mankind and decided to start all over again. He wanted Noah's help in repopulating the planet, so he warned Noah in advance that

"A fool gives full vent to his anger, but a wise man quietly holds it back

(Proverbs 29:11).

He was getting ready to flood the earth, destroy all the people and animals, and begin again. Noah built an ark to God's exact specifications and boarded it with his family and two animals from every species. Then God flooded the earth, wiped out every person and animal except those on the ark, and started over. But this was not the last time He did it.

Later, God felt a need to start over … again. But this time, instead of destroying the sinners, He destroyed sin and left Jesus behind as our Savior!

It all comes down to dwelling on something. And believe me when I tell you that unforgiveness builds up. No offense plus one offense equals an offense. You stew. Add one more offense, and now you have two offenses to brood over. Add one more offense and you have three offenses that will eat you alive. Before you know it, you're filled up with offenses against you, and you're an angry person with a short fuse. You have to constantly start over.

Be quick not to anger, for anger lodges in the bosom of fools

(Ecclesiastes 7:9).

Forgiveness leads to wisdom. You're free. You take the handbag and give it away when you forgive someone. You give the handbag to your offender. You don't forget that you've been wronged. That would be stupid. If you didn't remember what caused all the problems, you would walk right back into trouble again. No. You don't forget. You don't have to walk back into difficulty. But you have to forgive. When you forgive, you are free. The offense will still be in your mind. But it won't be your issue. It won't destroy you.

With an open spirit, free from anger and unforgiveness, there is nothing to hold you back from becoming a Spiritual Leader.

What if the person who made you mad was God? Is it okay to be angry with God? Yes! Of course. And when that happens, you need to forgive God. He doesn't need for you to forgive Him, but you need to do it for YOU.

And just in case you're having trouble getting motivated to forgive someone who's really hurt or offended you, please note that the Bible is very clear that unforgiveness has some pretty serious consequences for you. "For if you forgive men when they sin against you, your heavenly Father will also forgive you. But if you do not forgive men their sins, your Father will not forgive your sins" (Matthew 6:14, 15).

CORE ACTION

Think of someone who really ticked you off. Stop. Breathe in. (No, just kidding ... here's what to really do.) Ask yourself some questions:

Why am I so angry?

What's the value in hanging on to this anger?

How do I want this to turn out?

How can we make this moment better?

What will it take to bring justice back to you? Could it be God?

You know anger starts inside you. It's internalized. Then it manifests physically. It goes out. Bring it back in and deal with it. Right now.

Put it into God's hands. Give it to God. Put it down. Let it go.

Now forgive. This issue is now between your offender and God. You're free from it.

Do not take revenge, my friends, but leave room for God's wrath, for it is written: 'It is mine to avenge; I will repay,' says the Lord (Romans 12:19).

Above all, love each other deeply, because love covers a multitude of sins (1 Peter 4:8).

Love never fails (1 Corinthians 13:8).

Let all bitterness and wrath and anger and clamor and slander be put away from you, with all malice, and be kind to one another, tenderhearted, forgiving one another, as God in Christ forgave you (Ephesians 4:32, 32).

DEALING WITH ENVY

Jealousy is wanting something someone else has. Envy takes that to another level. (In Greek, it's translated as an "evil eye," with "eye" meaning a jealous sideglance.) There's negative action involved in envy. There's a resentment. For example, I might be jealous of another guy's truck. But when I'm envious, I might think about slashing his tires, so that he can't drive it anymore. Or if there's a guy who's better than I am in school, I might think about taking his notebook so that he can't do well on the next test. That's the difference between jealousy and envy. Envy has evil intent.

> ## For it is from within, from the human heart, that evil intentions come: fornication, theft, murder, adultery, avarice, wickedness, deceit, licentiousness, envy, slander, pride, folly
>
> (Mark 7:21-22 NRS).

Notice that envy is evil intention coming from *within the human heart*. It comes out as a manifestation of wrong.

People who are insecure can fall into envy. Envy is not a matter of another person having something you want, although it is a matter of something don't have. The thing you *don't* have is really a sense of how much you *do* have. In other words, you don't have any idea of your own worth. You have no idea of how valuable you are to the Maker who created you. Envy tries to create self-worth with possessions and physical looks. But that's not what you're worth. That's not who you are.

Even among Christians, we've seen envy over matters of spirituality. Someone might perceive himself as "having less God" than someone else. And that spawns envy. At SouthTown, we've actually seen a guy start rumors to undermine the leadership of a godly person. The envious guy couldn't stand it that "things" were working for his fellow Christian, and set about to destroy him in the name of God.

"These proclaim Christ out of love, knowing that I have been put here for the defense of the gospel; the others proclaim Christ out of selfish ambition, not sincerely but intending to increase my suffering in my imprisonment" (Philippians 1:15-17).

The way out of envy is to acknowledge that envy isn't about the other person. Forget what anybody else has or is. Imagine taking away all their stuff, their clothes, hair, abilities, and money ... and you'll discover that everybody is the same. All human. God looks at all of us as bare essentials with potential. So, how does that make them better than you? Doesn't.

So, you have to be content with yourself. God made you. God loves you enough to change the course of history. Enough to make BC and AD. Enough to die for you.

"For it was you who formed my inward parts; you knit me together in my mother's womb. I praise you, for I am fearfully and wonderfully made. Wonderful are your works; that I know very well. My frame was not hidden from you, when I was being made in secret, intricately woven in the depths of the earth. Your eyes beheld my unformed substance. In your book were written all the days that were formed for me, when none of them as yet existed" (Psalm 139:13-18).

Envy is not pleasing to God. He doesn't want us to compare ourselves with others or lift ourselves up. In fact, the Bible says that it's unwise (2 Corinthians 10:12). He made each of us as unique individuals, designed and planned by Him. It's not for you to disapprove of His judgment in gifting any of His children ... even you.

CORE ACTION

Next time you see a person you think has it all over you, remember that he or she was created by God just the way He wanted. Instead of envying, admire God's great creation. Thank Him for blessing that person. It's a hard thing to do, even for mature adults, but if you can get into the habit of appreciating God's work, you'll see miracles everywhere and you'll be happier with yourself.

I admit that I used to envy:

The reason is, that he (she) had _____, and I wanted and deserved it.

What a great job God did on:
I praise God and give Him the glory for the following things that he/she has and is:

I pray that God will continue to bless:

God is in
everything
and so you must
live for Him
in everything
that you do.

Nathan Abplanalp, Age 18

DEALING WITH PRIDE

You may have heard the phrase, "He takes pride in his work."
That sense of pride can be something positive, making you do your very best to achieve excellence, and where your efforts become a blessing to others (your parents, boss, etc,). But to be a *proud person* is a very negative attribute. It is when you think much too highly of yourself and your achievements or accomplishments, and this type of pride is definitely sin. And when you boast about yourself, it really doesn't count for much. "For it is not the one who commends himself who is approved, but the one who the Lord commends." (2 Corinthians 10:18). It's much better to let someone else praise you for your achievements than for you to broadcast them all over town.

Arrogance is pride's twin. It is when you start judging other people based on your own achievement. You think, "I'm better than that guy." The Bible says in Proverbs 16:18 that "Pride goes before destruction and a haughty (proud or arrogant) spirit before a fall."

There was a guy that used to wakeboard with us that was having a phenomenal day. He was riding great! But the next day when he came to ride, he had arrogance "written all over him." We prayed to God that he would have a bad day so he wouldn't be caught in that terrible pride trap. And it happened! He couldn't do anything right, and fell numerous times. He was humbled. We need to remember that Jesus was "better" than His disciples, but *He* served *them.* He wasn't the Son of God in arrogance. He was the Son in humility.

When you are humble, you are willing to share your achievements with others. Suppose you are super smart in biology, for example. The person at your lab table just can't seem to dissect that piglet. They can't do the lab report because they just can't even figure out if it is a male or female specimen. Instead of making fun of their lack of ability or just ignoring them, you help them and share your knowledge. (Of course, I don't mean cheating.)

Arrogance, however, is holding your achievements to yourself for your own benefit. You focus on your own stuff.

Pride can be an instantaneous feeling when you accomplish something, but one that quickly fades when you realize there's more and better, and you still haven't gone big enough. But pride's also a creeper. First you're prideful, then you're boastful. It builds in intensity. Slowly you see your separation from others. You're no longer equal but better.

Pride also removes your joy. How social can you be when you're arrogant? You stop learning when you're proud because you develop an unteachable spirit. You stop asking for help. And pretty soon you'll find yourself defending your pride and justifying yourself. You can no longer admit limitations. You can't be wrong anymore. What a miserable existence! "By pride comes nothing but strife." (Proverbs 13:10)

Pride and arrogance, like all sin, separate us from the presence of God. "God resists the proud, but gives grace to the humble." (I Peter 5:5)

CORE ACTION

Find something you're proud of, and then find someone who is better at it than you are. Realize that you're not all that great. Get rid of pride and become a servant.

Find someone who is not as good at a certain skill as you are. Help him/her to reach your level. (Love your neighbor as yourself).

Next time you try something, ask God to help you. This way when you achieve it, (and you will) you will be clear about who gets the credit. As you give the glory to God, you will be able to achieve even more. You'll go bigger.

Proverbs 16:18 that "Pride goes before destruction and a haughty (proud or arrogant) spirit before a fall."

Erin's Story

At fifteen I hated school; I could feel myself growing old as I sat through each class. Outside of class was almost worse. Everyone would always ask how school was going, and where was I planning to go to college. One night I sat down to contemplate my life. I would graduate at seventeen, go to college (more school) for four years, graduate at twenty-one, get a job, and die before I had lived. That was it. I decided I was not going to

I realized that God rarely calls you to where you feel comfortable.

Erin Easter

I found myself 'babysitting' every Friday night... holding someone's hair back while she vomited.

college. I wanted to travel. I wanted to make my own decisions, to be tied to nothing, and live.

I met Jesus at a very young age. I had a deep faith, and we hung out a lot. I know that sounds strange, but I've always had a unique relationship with the Lord, built on openness and honesty. So, that night, I took my fears to the Lord. I stayed up for hours telling God how I thought school was pointless, I couldn't believe someone would go voluntarily for an extra four years, but everyone expected me to go as well. We talked for hours. I cried and just shared my heart with Him. Then I began the most important part of prayer... I listened. I didn't hear God in some loud, audible voice, or even read it in the Bible, but as I lay in bed that night I felt His peace. I realized what I already knew: He would take care of me; my fears were petty. I simply knew that if I served Him and lived for the Lord, I wouldn't be disappointed.

But I still wasn't going to college. By my junior year in high school, I was planning to move to Costa Rica when I graduated. I had no idea what I would do there; it just sounded far from the confines of school and very exciting. In reality, I had no direction, I had no idea what I was going to do with my life, and as my senior year approached, that is all anyone wanted to know.

Towards the end of my senior year, still Costa Rica bound, I remembered that conversation I had with the Lord my freshman year. I realized that in the past three years, I had traveled out of the country, and had been on plenty of road trips. I realized that Jesus had kept His end of the deal, and I needed to go to college. Now the question had become which one.

I didn't live exactly like everyone in high school. I didn't drink, had never done drugs, and I felt like I

had to be the last remaining virgin in the western hemisphere. But I hated to miss out; I was at every party, every game, every event. I didn't have too many friends who partied sober. I found myself 'babysitting' every Friday night— holding someone's hair back while she vomited, helping someone down the stairs, and always driving. I decided I was tired of the scene and didn't want to spend the next four years (or five as it turned out) at that same party. I knew there were better ways to celebrate. So, after visiting a few Christian colleges, I decided to attend Lee University in Cleveland, Tennessee. It wasn't Costa Rica, but it was five hours away from my small town, so it was just far enough for me.

It's amazing how hard it is to please people. My parents were pretty relieved that I was not only in the country, but also in college. That should have been enough, but the insatiable question came next: "What's your major?" It might as well be your last name at school, "Hi I'm Josh, Political Science" "Hi I'm Erin, Undecided." It took me this long to decide where I would be for four years; now I was expected to know what I wanted to do with the rest of my life! Are you kidding me? The process of elimination didn't help. I hate science, can't sing, was not blessed with the coordination needed for athletics, have no teaching ability, and history bores me out of my mind. I considered business, but after one seminar filled with international business majors, my idea of the business world was formalities, panty hose, selfishness, and love for money. That was not for me. So, by my junior year in college I had taken eighteen hours of electives (which are classes that don't actually count), and it was time to choose a major. Man, God and I wrestled on that one. Now don't get me wrong. I didn't go against God. I didn't fight, but I protested. We wrestled; I lost. God told me I had to be a business major. Again, it was just something I knew; everything else felt wrong, and I had a peace about business … even if I didn't like it.

This is a funny thing about God that I was starting to realize: He rarely calls you to where you feel comfortable. I think He gets more glory when we do something we don't want to out of obedience and then realize we love it and glorify Him. The point is that I became, "Erin, Business Administration." Yes, I know, very interesting ... right.

Each summer I would head home, and right to the lake. I even waited tables at night so that I could be out wakeboarding during the days. Mikie and I would go out every day with Andy or anyone else who wanted to ride. Mikie eventually moved in with Danny and Owen, and that's when the wakeboarding got serious. It's also when the boys got serious. One of the best phone calls I've ever received came during the fall of my sophomore year. It started out as heart-wrenching; Mikie told me that we had lost a friend after a party. He went on to say that he had 'slowed down' in the party scene and had gone to church with Danny. He went straight into how he, Danny, and Owen were going to go on tour, wakeboarding and telling kids about Christ! After we hung up, it took a minute to sink in; then I ran to the bathroom and told my roommates that Mike had gotten saved, and we all screamed!

That winter the boys were out on the lake so often they earned a name for themselves: The SouthTown Riders, which later titled the vision, SouthTown Riders, Inc. I was excited and supportive of the vision of SouthTown; we were constantly batting ideas around and contemplating next steps toward the reality. I was home on break when Danny approached me about joining SouthTown. A four-member board is required for incorporation. Danny, Mikie, and David only made three. I remember Danny pointing out that I was a business major and that I would be educated on the business side of SouthTown, an aspect that they "didn't want to deal with." I prayed, and I knew this was where I belonged. I found my niche.

God took care of every one of my fears

It's overwhelming to me that the last things I wanted to do were the very things that got me to where I am suppose to be. Had I not gone to college and then majored in business, I wouldn't be involved with SouthTown right now. God took care of every one of my fears, even the petty ones. College really was the best five, yes five, years of my life. I made the best friends I will ever know, was blessed with wise and caring professors, and I have traveled to over 13 different countries since high school. And even though I became a *stuffy* business major, I get to tell kids about Jesus, mentor teenage girls, and wakeboard endlessly ... and I haven't worn a pair of panty hose since I graduated college!

ERIN EASTER

Graduating high school brings pressure, and college brings even more, but with God in control, it all works out. I know I would have had a hard time believing that my freshman year of high school, but that's why faith is so important. When you really feel that pressure, go with what you already know—that God is good and He keeps His promises. You don't always have to feel the pressure of making the right decision, because when you are obedient to the Lord, it removes the chance that you could make the wrong one.

You don't always have to feel the pressure of making the right decision, because when you are obedient to the Lord, it removes the chance that you could make the wrong one.

**Godly sorrow brings repentance
that leads to salvation and
leaves no regret, but
worldly sorrow brings death.**

(2 Corinthians 7:10)

Guilt

When you do something wrong, you have this feeling of shame and regret and of wanting to somehow make it right. You feel awful. But guilt, as defined by the Greeks, is not a feeling. It's a **debt**. It's something you owe someone. Okay, so maybe that debt might be an apology or replacing something you broke or accepting some sort of punishment, but beyond that, guilt is not what you think it is.

So let guilt go. No emotional meltdown. No beating yourself up. God forgives you.

To understand guilt is to understand why Jesus died. We walk in forgiveness, not condemnation.

"Godly sorrow brings repentance that leads to salvation and leaves no regret, but worldly sorrow brings death" (2 Corinthians 7:10).

Of course, guilt (as a feeling) serves a (very small) useful purpose in your life. It tells you that your conscience is still very much alive, that you have honor, and that you know the difference between right and wrong … and you want to do "right." Doing wrong grieves you. Guilt drives you to repent, meaning that you feel sorrow and ask for forgiveness. And more than that, you usually vow to NEVER do the guilt-causing thing again. Ever. Quickly take the whole thing to God in prayer, and once all that's done, move on. God loves you. You're forgiven. Jesus paid your debt.

CORE ACTION

Think of someone you've wronged. Maybe you've disobeyed or been disrespectful to your parents. First, ask God to forgive you. Then, apologize to your parents and ask them to forgive you. Finally, pay the penalty thankfully. In other words, pay your debt by doing whatever it is that they wanted you to do. This way, you all win. God is pleased. Your folks are pleased. And you're off the hook in the guilt department.

Here's a quick example. Maybe they asked you to clean your room. You refused. They were angry. Things aren't good between you now. Go to God and ask His forgiveness for being a disobedient, disrespectful son or daughter. Then go to your parents, apologize, and ask their forgiveness. (They'll be shocked!) Finally, go and clean your room better than it's ever been cleaned.

That might have been a bit time consuming, but it was simple, right? Sometimes being forgiven our debt by a person and getting free from guilt can seem not quite so easy.

What happens if the person you've wronged will not forgive you? (It happens!) Well, remember that you ask God's forgiveness FIRST. He forgives if you're sincerely sorry. Now, you go to the person you've wronged and ask forgiveness, and he or she says, "No way." It doesn't matter. The most important forgiveness has already taken place: God's.

And here's the other important thing that has happened: You told the truth and made it right. To get free from guilt, you have to pay a penalty—make something right and clear the debt. At this point, it's less about making the person happy. It's more about your doing what you have to do to clear the debt. Once you've done all you can to make it right, and you've asked for forgiveness from God and the person you've wronged, you're clear. Guilt is no longer your handbag.

Notes on giving guilt the heave-ho:

I wronged _____ by doing the following:

How guilt has felt to me:

How I paid my debt:

How it feels to be forgiven:

The hardest part of this was:

Notes for next time:

God not only acts through church activities; He helps me to live day by day and not be afraid of the future.

Taylor Hoynacki, Age 14

As I grow in my faith, I realize how much He works around us every day.

Adam Greer, age 21

Why Peter?

I have always been interested in the stories in the Bible that have to do with Jesus and His disciples. I have always been fascinated with Peter as being one of Jesus' closest disciples. He is set apart from all the rest by the name that Jesus gave him: "Peter."

The simple meaning of the name Peter is "Rock." We all know rocks to be hard and solid. If you stomp on one, it will most likely hurt you before you can crush it. The only real way to destroy a rock is to pound at it little by little with a hammer and chisel or totally destroy it with a sledge hammer ...or for the really big ones, dynamite.

Peter was to have the properties of a rock. Strong and solid, he would be the foundation for the church to be built upon. Couldn't Jesus have picked a better man than Peter? I have no answer to that question. The only thing I can tell you is that He did pick Peter, and Peter tried his hardest to live up to his name.

It actually gives me encouragement that Jesus would pick someone like Peter. If we think about a lot of Peter's actions, we can see that he really doesn't get the whole picture that Jesus has set before him. At some moments, he can be the most faithful of disciples, claiming that he would die for his Lord. In the next moment, he turns around and denies Jesus three times. He can step out on the water, a huge act of trust and faith, and then get distracted and sink right back down into the water.

Peter had Jesus' divinity revealed to him in so many ways, and he would still turn around and question Jesus, enough so that Jesus would even have to say, "Get thee behind me Satan!" God spoke into his ear on the mountain of transfiguration (the mountain that Jesus took three disciples up and where He began to shine and glow with a radiance from heaven). God told him, "Jesus is my Son." A statement that declares Jesus is divine—let's not forget the glowing either.

Okay, we can establish that Peter has some very definite character flaws when it comes to understanding God and following His commands, but how much are we really like Peter? I know in my life

I don't always get what God is trying to get me to do. I also know that I too have great faith sometimes, and then I can simply get distracted and sink right down into the water. How true is this for you?

We get excited when God provides and can't even comprehend His provision, but when things get tight, we turn around and worry about money. Peter did this also; he saw all the people fed on the mountainside and then worried about how he would pay a tax. Jesus would have to tell him to cut a fish open, that the money for his taxes was inside. Jesus always was one step ahead of him.

In a sense, we are all like Peter. We are with Jesus, sometimes very close to Him and sometimes distant. As believers we are called to follow Him. Belief (or faith) itself is to recognize the divinity of Jesus. Sometime we make Jesus our Lord and sometimes He is made out to be just another homeboy. Some may have even denied Jesus like Peter had. But Jesus is always one step ahead of us.
Before Jesus left Peter's presence, after He was raised from the dead, He asked Peter a series of questions. "Do you love me?" He asked three times, and each time used a different word for love. Each time the word grew stronger. It was the third time that Peter ends his reply with, "Lord, you know all things, you know that I love you." Peter is acknowledging that Jesus knows his heart, and that in the depths of himself, Jesus knows he loves Him. Jesus asked Peter for his account of love, but Peter's final answer was given with his heart.

CORE ACTION

Now that Christ is looking at you, He will ask you," Do you love me?" Will your ultimate answer be from your lips or will it be heard by Jesus because your heart speaks it?

Could you express love both ways?

How will you say it with your heart? In your prayers?

How will you say it in your actions?

You live this real. Wakeboarding is my worship. Being a Christian is a great responsibility. I was found wanting but I have it now.

Matt Hemric, age 18

The Moment of Salvation

You know the hymn, *Amazing Grace*? There's a line in it that says, "Amazing Grace, how sweet the sound that saved a wretch like me." But what does being "saved" mean?

Salvation (saving) means being saved from hell. It's the promise of heaven. It's an ongoing process from the time of hearing ("So then faith comes by hearing and hearing by the Word of God" Romans 10:17.) to the time of death. After death, it's truly complete. In Scripture, the establishment of salvation can be found from the very first verse in the Old Testament to the last verse in the New Testament. Yet there is a "moment of salvation" that we experience when we leave the "old self" behind and put on a "new self."

> Therefore if anyone is in Christ, he is a new creation: old things have passed away; behold, all things have become new.
>
> **(2 Corinthians 5:17)**

But how do we do this? How do we become a "new person?"

In the Old Testament days people had to bring sacrifices to the temple and repent of their sins on a regular basis to get back in right standing with God after they had broken the law. They did this until the day they died. However, in the New Testament during the time of Christ, people received direct forgiveness of their sins from Jesus Himself. ("Then He said to her, 'Your sins are forgiven.'" Luke 7:48) This business of forgiveness is one reason the religious leaders had such a problem with Jesus. He was breaking their tradition of sacrificial offerings as the means of forgiveness. "And those who sat at the table with Him began to say to themselves, 'Who is this who even forgives sins?'" (Luke 7:49). Or in other words, "Who does he think he is, forgiving sins like this?"

But Jesus is not on earth today, so how are *our* sins forgiven?

Romans 10:9 answers that question. "That if you confess with your mouth the Lord Jesus and believe in your heart that God has raised Him from the dead, you will be saved."

"Saved from what?" is a common question we get at SouthTown as we are witnessing to people. As I said earlier, the answer is simple: saved from hell, the eternal separation from God.

Now, let's break this verse down.

The first part, "confessing with your mouth," is a direct reference to outwardly acknowledging that Jesus is Lord. This confession is your action. It is when you openly recognize Jesus as the Lord of your life and proclaim that you belong to Him and that He is God. He now gives the orders and you obey His will instead of your own.

"Believing in your heart that God raised Him from the dead" is more than just an emotional feeling. The Greek word for "belief" is *pistis*, and it means "to have faith in" and "to put your trust in." It is a mode of thinking. As humans, we trust the truth. We have faith in things that are truthful. "Believing," then, is the internal and intellectual establishment that Jesus Christ died and was resurrected by God. It is when we form the conclusion in our hearts and minds that the resurrection is an absolute truth. Without the resurrection, salvation would be impossible.

Romans 10:9 clearly teaches that confessing His Lordship and believing in His resurrection are what we need to be saved and have eternal life, to be "born again" and "start brand new."

It is actually only *after* we recognize Jesus as Lord that our sins are forgiven (Acts 10:43). And the forgiveness of sin *is* the evidence of salvation (Luke 1:77).

The woman in Luke chapter 7 was a sinner who poured expensive oil on Jesus' feet as she cried and washed His feet with her tears. While others were complaining about her, Jesus told her that her sins were forgiven and that her faith had saved her. She didn't first ask Him to forgive her for her sins. Yet Jesus did just that. He forgave her because He knew she had recognized who He was and that she had believed in Him. Her actions were her way of confessing Him as Lord, and this confession brought forgiveness. That was her moment of salvation.

CORE ACTION

This Core Action is going to take some time. You're going to have to pray and read the Bible, but we'll help you to figure out how.

Maybe you have never thought much about who Jesus *really* is. Or maybe you have asked Him to forgive you many times, but have failed to truly recognize Him as the resurrected Lord, *your* Lord, and so you still are struggling with the same sins. He wants you to know Him. He wants you to receive forgiveness. He is faithful to answer all who call out to Him.

In prayer, ask Jesus Christ to reveal Himself to you.

Read about Him and see what He says firsthand in the Gospels. (Matthew, Mark, Luke and John in the New Testament part of the Bible). Read carefully. You'll especially enjoy the four points of view about the life and teaching of Christ: how those points of view are alike and how they're a little different, and when they're combined, how they bring you deep understanding.

If you need help in your search for Truth, the SouthTown team is here for you. Just e-mail us: Godstuff@southtownriders.com

Jesus said, "I am the way, the truth and the life. No man comes to the Father except through Me." John 14:6

As a boarder, I want to take it as far as God will let me go. Try to live every day the best I can and keep God involved in everything I do.

Anndrew Smith, Age 18

Meredith's Story

I always told myself that I was not going to college to get my MRS. Degree. I definitely did not want to just date one guy. I wanted to flirt with lots of guys, get lots of free dinners, and just enjoy the single life. I knew I wanted to focus on school and my relationship with Christ, and I didn't want the distraction of a serious or steady boyfriend. That was not exactly how things worked out …

Meeting David

I walked onto the lawn in Alumni Park, looking forward to meeting new people, never thinking I would be meeting lifelong friends. I started talking to a couple of guys who said they were from Charlotte, North Carolina. That wasn't far from my own hometown, so I felt like we had a connection. After realizing that David, Kevin and I had more in common, I decided that I had found some cool friends to hang out with during the next two weeks while at the Summer Honors Program at Lee University.

The program was designed for high school juniors and seniors to come to Lee for a "real college experience," including dorm life, cafeteria food, hanging out and even classes—two of

We humans are capable of a lot more than we think.

Meredith Tolentino

them—for three hours every day. Not exactly a realistic take on college life, but close enough to get a student hooked!

The three of us actually had both classes together, so we ended up hanging out a lot. One night we were going to see the Dixie Stampede, a rodeo type dinner theatre, and I realized that I was really enjoying getting to know David. We had so much in common and yet at the same time were opposite in many ways. I felt like David was different than any guy I had ever met. Maybe it was his crazy hair, his creativity, or his love for God, but I knew I wanted to hang out with him more.

We had lots of long talks about everything from knowing a person's salvation to our dreams for the future. He told me about wakeboarding and doing mime. I learned that he was from the Dominican Republic, which is where I had been the previous summer on a mission's trip. I just couldn't explain it, but I knew that there was something different about him. And I had an inkling that he felt the same way about me.

The two weeks passed quickly, yet it seemed like I knew so much about this guy … I couldn't wait to get to see him again!

Before I knew it, school had started and I was in a tiny room in a dorm, taking exams, eating cafeteria food, and loving college life. David and I had really become good friends and although I knew there was something more, I didn't want to push it. After all, we were just freshmen, and there was no need to get serious with literally the first guy I had met from Lee! But, as life would have it, I couldn't keep myself from falling in love with him. We decided in that first semester that there was no need to pretend we weren't exclusively dating each other, so we officially became a couple.

Our First Christmas Together
That Christmas my parents actually let me spend Christmas day with David's family! I was amazed because my family is close-knit and we always spend the holidays together. But I was excited by the new freedom. We hung out with David's parents, his brother Danny, his sister Becky, and her husband Eric. It was both weird and wonderful at the same time, because I felt like I was already a part of this new family.

The day after Christmas, the boys had the great idea of going out on the lake to wakeboard! I thought they were crazy, but I've always loved boats and the water, so I piled on my ski clothes to stay warm and followed David. Danny and David both prepared to ride by putting on their snowboard gear and their dry suits on top of that. They had the winter wakeboarding thing down to a science. They filled up an ice cooler with hot water and placed it in the boat for immediate use when a rider completed his run and needed to warm his hands and feet.

At the lake we met up with this little kid, Austin, and his dad, who joined us on Danny's boat. I thought his dad had brought Austin out to watch the boys ride, but I was shocked when Austin himself got in and started doing tricks! For being a little 12-year-old, Austin was really good! The funniest part was that because Austin was so small, after riding, instead of just warming up his hands and feet in the hot water cooler, he would just get inside!

Later that day we went to pick up one of Danny's friends, Mike, and his sister. He was a really good rider, and I was so impressed with what he could do! It was crazy to watch all these guys ride—especially in the middle of the winter when the temperature was freezing and there was ice on the lake! I knew then that David was definitely committed to this sport of wakeboarding!

First Attempt to Wakeboard
When spring arrived, we went home for a long weekend and David finally made me try this wakeboarding thing. I had seen him do it so many times, but I was too scared to try it myself. But he kept telling me how much I would love it, so before I could think twice, I found myself attached to a board with just a handle in my hands. The boat was taking off, and I was doing my best to trail behind as I tried to get my balance on top of the water. I was pretty nervous, especially since everyone else in the boat that day was so good! But as soon as I realized

Before I could think twice, I found myself attached to a board with just a handle in my hands.

it was something that I could actually do, I relaxed and really started to enjoy myself! Just one glimpse into wakeboarding, and I now could understand why David was so crazy about this sport, and I decided that I had it in me to be crazy about it too!

The "One"

As summer came around, David and I worked at a camp at Lee. It was a music, art and drama camp, and David and I were "volunteered" to work the drama section. Middle and high school students came to this camp, and as things go, we got all the middle school boys in our group. We had to choreograph a drama to a song … and that's just not the easiest thing to do with middle school boys! Not to mention, it had to be good enough to perform in a church service only two days later! So, as I struggled with my perfectionist tendencies to get these students ready, David awed me with how well he could enjoy what he was doing, get the students to do what he wanted, and help them have fun all at the same time. And I was pleasantly surprised with how well we worked as a team. Our kids worked so hard to get the drama together and we were so proud of them!

People always talk about finding "the one" to marry and how you know when you *have* found him. This weekend was it for me. I saw David as this amazing man of God that worked so tirelessly and effortlessly with middle schoolers—

which we all know can be a feat! I realized that I wanted to be a part of whatever God had in store for him and that was it. I just knew from that weekend on that he was the man that I was going to marry.

My Beginnings with SouthTown

As we began our sophomore year of college, our lives were getting more adjusted to each other and to the future that we would have together. David and Danny had been discussing pioneering a ministry based around wakeboarding. At that time, I didn't understand how I would fit in (because I am not a great wakeboarder), but somehow I just knew God would work it out.

That fall, David got a phone call from Danny telling us that Mike and another wakeboarder, Andy, had given their lives to Christ and were getting involved at David's home church. It seemed as if God, at just the right time, brought just the right people together, and the dream of SouthTown Riders began to become a reality.

Not long after, Danny shared with David that the only way to make this ministry work was to be a non-profit organization. Well, my dad is a CPA, but on the side, he sets up non-profits! I gave him a call, and he said he would help SouthTown out. All the pieces were coming together.

Things were taking off with SouthTown and David started to work during the school year on designing the necessary graphics for the new ministry. He even built a computer with one of his roommates so that he would have the technological capacity that the work would require.

A proposal. . .

It was time for yet another Christmas—our junior Christmas. David's parents were taking both of us up to New York City to go see family and some of their closest friends. This was only my second trip to New York City, but I was thrilled, knowing that I was going with people who actually knew the city!

On the flight up to New York, I had been reading a book that David's mom had written. It was his parents' story about their mission field experiences. The chapter I was engrossed in was the account of the time his dad proposed to his mom at the famous Radio City Music Hall. I'm sure this place held special memories for them, and it all seemed very romantic. Tonight would be my first time visiting Radio City, and reading their story just added to my excitement as

I thought about the show we would see—the Christmas Music Spectacular with the Radio City Rockettes.

We arrived in New York City in the afternoon and enjoyed walking around Manhattan and taking in all the Christmas sights. In the evening, I found myself standing in the very beautiful and prestigious Radio City Music Hall. We had gotten there a little early, so David and I stayed in the lobby to look around, enjoy the building, and just people-watch. We were standing in the second floor lobby, overlooking the first, and David started talking about how special this place was for his mom and dad. "I want this to be a special place for us too," I remember him saying. I told him it already was special for us because we were there together. But I was soon to find out that he had a little more in mind! We were standing shoulder to shoulder and I could feel his heart beating through his arm. Then I heard a box pop and *my* heart started racing.

"Surely he was not about to propose because he had so adamantly explained that he did not have enough money for a ring yet," my mind argued as a million thoughts simultaneously raced through my head. Yet the next thing I knew, David had taken my hand and slid it into his coat pocket and gently slipped a ring on my finger.

In my ear he whispered, "Will you marry me?"

In my ear he whispered, "Will you marry me?" My response? Well, not the one that I always thought I would have in this moment, you know, with the tears and everything. I could not process how all this had been put together without me finding out! There was not a slip from anyone, and *everyone* knew but me!

I looked at David, and in my state of shock, I bluntly asked, "Did you ask my dad?" I know, not the romantic way to answer, but I just could not quite comprehend that this was *the* proposal! After he laughed at me and said that he had my dad's blessings, I came to my senses enough to say, "Of course, I'll marry you!" A small kiss in that private lobby sealed the exciting event and we walked happily back into the theater just in time for the show to begin. Needless to say, I don't quite remember too much of the show… I was a little distracted by a new piece of jewelry on my finger and the man that would officially now soon be my husband!

Afterwards, David and his parents laughed about the irony that only this morning I had been reading about his dad's proposal in the exact same place! The rest of the trip, David got to introduce me to his family and special friends as his fiancé, which was a beautiful sound to my ears.

A Tough Semester

The next semester was definitely one of my toughest ever. All the excitement of planning my wedding got a bit distanced when my grandfather passed away in January. A quick trip home to sing at the funeral and be with family was foreshadowing for the rest of the semester.

On Valentine's Day the next month, my other grandfather passed away. Another quick trip home to sing in a funeral, comfort family and get back to school to try to catch up on the accumulating days I was missing.

If I have not mentioned up until this point, I was a voice major in school. Sometime in February, I noticed this large lump in the back of my throat near my tonsils. It was uncomfortable and very strange, so I went to a local doctor to have it checked out, and he recommended a specialist in my hometown because he felt it needed someone with more knowledge. So, another flight home to have this lump checked out, and I found out that it needed to be removed. Surgery was scheduled for my spring break the following month because I knew I could not afford to miss any more school—especially since this was one of my most demanding scholastic semesters.

It was God's strength that got me through that time in my life.

Spring break came quickly and I went in for throat surgery. The doctors didn't know what the mass was, but once they removed it, they determined it was a benign tumor. Praise God that it wasn't cancer, and they didn't even hurt my vocal chords in the surgery!

So, just when I thought that I had gotten through the rough times of the semester, my great-grandmother passed away in April. I think her death is what really "did me in" for the semester. I got the news right before my very tough music history class, and when I went in to tell my professor, I just started uncontrollably crying! I always had prided myself on being able to keep control, but Meme's passing away was my breaking point. Up until now, I had almost become numb to all that I had been through with deaths and surgery—almost like a routine: come home, go to a funeral or have surgery, go back to school, and never deal with my emotions because I had to function at school to make the grades I needed to keep my scholarship. I hadn't taken the time to process the changes that had

occurred in my life and in my family over the past three months. Even when I came home for Meme's funeral, and sang at it, and spent time with family, I still went back to school numb to the ordeal.

I didn't actually take the time to deal with me—my emotions, my pain, and just letting the Lord take care of me, until sometime that following summer. I had been staying strong for my parents, so I had just tucked all my grief away in this corner of my heart in a place labeled "deal with later." Poor David definitely felt the weight of my stress that semester because I took it out on him. He was so great in that he just held me so many times when that was all that I needed—a tangible person. I knew that God had given me David that semester to be a concrete expression of His love for me. I know that God's timing is impeccable and that His word says that He will never let us be tempted beyond what we can bear, but that He will always provide a way out (I Corinthians 10:13). He gave me the strength I needed that semester to be strong for my family and to keep the

GPA that I needed for my scholarship, and provided special friends who supported me when I needed it most. I learned a lot from that semester—we humans are capable of a lot more than we think. Looking back, if someone had told me ahead of time that all those tragedies would have occurred in a row within four months, I don't think I would have believed them, or believed that I had the strength to hold up through it. But good thing I didn't have to rely on my own strength—it was God's strength that got me through that time in my life.

Hearing Praise Reports from Afar

It seemed like every time David heard from Danny during our senior year, it was another miracle, another praise report, or just something amazing that God was doing to provide and prepare SouthTown for ministry that summer. The coolest phone call of that year was the one when Danny said, "Supra came through, and we're going to be getting TWO FREE boats for this summer!" We were so excited, yet it didn't seem real because we were so far away. All we could do was just praise God for the way He was moving back home.

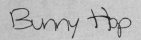

Bunny Hop

Cut out on your heel side edge. As you get to the end of your cut, push down with your front foot. Then quickly push down hard with your back foot. As you feel your board coming off the water you should pull your knees up to your chest. The harder you push off the water with your feet and the higher you pull up your knees, the bigger your Ollie or Bunny Hop will be!

MEREDITH TOLENTINO

It was really tough to be in Tennessee at Lee University while God was moving so mightily back in Charlotte. But the cool thing God was teaching both David and me was that we were in a preparation stage—a time of waiting. It definitely was not the most fun place to be, but we were learning things that we were going to need to be in the ministry, and He had divinely appointed that time away from Charlotte. That preparation stage in life is so important. It is sometimes painful and frustrating, but the rewards are so fulfilling when it's over. God's timing is perfect, and although David and I knew that, we still had to go through that test of being away, of learning, growing, and being prepared for what was to come.

Last Semester of Lee . . .

The last semester of my life at Lee was filled with everything from wedding plans to my senior recital, as well as directing a pageant that Lee puts on every year. To say the least, it was busy. . . but not impossible. I had a really easy class load that semester, so I was having fun being involved in all those things.

Meanwhile, life at SouthTown was still taking off and coming together for the first summer of full time camps everyday. Danny and Mike had been going to churches throughout this semester, booking youth groups to come out to our clinics. Things were progressing very well.

SouthTown

David and I headed home in February for a SouthTown meeting. At this prayer meeting, Danny was talking about who would be working that upcoming summer at the camps. Up until this point, I thought I would be supporting David behind the scenes and helping when I could, but having another job entirely separate from SouthTown. The Lord prompted something in me when Danny was talking and I knew that I was supposed to work for SouthTown that summer, which was scary and required much trust, because SouthTown could not guarantee any financial reimbursement for my services. I prayed about it, and talked to David, my parents, and Danny. With their confirmation, I was convinced I was supposed to work for SouthTown when the summer started. The Lord has ways of instilling in you this undeniable peace when you walk in the path He has designed for you. There was not this huge voice that yelled in my ear, but it was this gentle tug at my heart strings that told me, "Yes, Meredith, I want you to work for SouthTown this summer." He didn't tell me it would be for one year, two years or ten years. He just said, this summer. I think the Lord is so good to just let us see a little bit in front of us. If we could see the whole picture—or even five years ahead—I think we would become overwhelmed, but it is the gentle whisper in our hearts that confirms not only the steps ahead, but pieces of our dreams as well.

water and fire

Graduation finally arrived. We had certainly grown through those four years at school; we were definitely not the same people that we were when we met. We had matured in our relationship together, but more importantly, in our relationship with Christ. A picture-perfect wedding shortly followed graduation, and then we found ourselves with an amazing journey ahead of us, with a faithful Master to guide and direct us each step of the way. And that journey would take us through the "water and fire" as we dedicated our lives in service to God at SouthTown Riders.

When you pass through the waters, I will be with you; and when you pass through the rivers, they will not sweep over you. When you walk through the fire, you will not be burned; the flames will not set you ablaze. Isaiah 43:2

Fire and Water

From its early beginnings, when wakeboarding was the primary sport of this ministry, SouthTown Riders adopted Isaiah 43:2-3 as its theme verse. It's written across the bow of every boat. "When you pass through the waters, I will be with you," can take on significant meaning whether you are being pulled on a wakeboard for the very first time or doing extreme maneuvers in a world competition! But this verse has been a lot more to the team than just a "protective covering" when out on the lake. It has been the comfort through hard times, the hope when things seemed impossible. Let's examine it further.

Water and fire are very different elements, and yet have striking similarities. Water, for example, can either be gas, as in the morning mist on the lake, liquid, as the lake itself, or solid, as in a block of ice (or how it feels sometimes during a bad fall!). Fire, on the other hand, has only one state: hot. It may have degrees of "hotness" according to the particular fuel being burned, but it is always hot and can never be cold. Both fire and water are necessary for life. Our bodies cannot survive very long without water before dehydration sets in. And food could hardly be cooked without fire. Yet they also have dangerous and deadly natures. You can drown in water even if you are a good swimmer, and no human can withstand the heat of fire without being burned severely or killed.

Jesus said that He was the "living water" and the Holy Spirit is sometimes referred to as "fire." Both of these are positive parallels, meaning that He quenches our "spiritual thirst," and His Spirit within us fuels our very life. Yet Isaiah 43:2-3 deals with both fire and water as destructive, able to snuff life from us. Rivers that overflow us, fires that burn us.

We all have experienced the type of problems that emotionally build up like a rising river, where we feel so stressed that we can't seem to keep our head above water. It could be after a prolonged sickness when the make-up work upon returning to school seems totally impossible to complete. Or it could be the "hard" side of water, where we face the death of a close friend or a member of our family.

No matter what we go through, Jesus is with us.

Some of the roughest moments the disciples had were on the water, but Jesus was always with them. He may have appeared to be asleep in the boat in the middle of the storm, but He was there. He may have come walking on the top and been mistaken for a ghost, but He was there. He calmed the water, and He calmed His disciples.

Sometimes Jesus used the water to teach his disciples, as when He tested Peter's trust in Him by asking Peter to step out of the boat and also walk on the water. Sometimes He will use the "raging sea" in our lives to teach us some great lessons. But the one thing we can count on is that He is with us.

Fire, unlike water, which can slowly rise and overtake us, is just plain hot and does immediate damage. It is the kind of trouble we face when something takes us by surprise. It could be suddenly finding out that our best friend has betrayed us, an unexpected doctor's report, a deadly car accident, or any trouble that we weren't expecting, but is devastating.

There is the famous story in the Bible in Daniel chapter 3 of three teenagers who were being punished for their obedience to God. They were thrown into a fiery furnace that was so hot that the guards who threw them in dropped dead from the heat. When the king went later to check on them, he was shocked to find them walking around in the fire with a fourth person with them. "Look!" he answered, "I see four men loose, walking in the midst of the fire; and they are not hurt, and the form of the fourth is like the Son of God" (Daniel 3:25). God Himself rescued them.

And that's what Isaiah 43: 2-3 is all about. The Lord always lets us know His hand is on us, whether we pass through treacherous waters or the hottest fire. No matter what we go through, Jesus is with us, and that gives birth to hope in our hearts. So don't fret when the hard times come. The bright side is that sooner or later the waters will calm, and fire can only burn so long before it is extinguished.

Remember Who has you!

CORE ACTION

List some things you are struggling with and divide them into two categories; water and fire.

In the "water" column list problems that have begun gradually and then have become overpowering and seemingly insurmountable. In the fire column, list things you have faced that had a sudden onset with devastating consequences.

WATER   FIRE

How did you face each one of these situations?

Were you aware of God being with you through the fire and through the water? How did you know?

... in quietness and confidence shall be your strength ...

(Isaiah 30:15)

Silence and the Power of Meditation:
Decision-Making

Before Christ did anything big, He went alone to pray in conversation with His Father.

Before He chose His disciples, He went to the mountain alone and prayed for guidance (Luke 6:12).

Before He walked on water, He had sent the disciples off in a boat and had gone up to the mountain to pray (Matthew 14:23 and Mark 4:46).

Before He went to His death on the Cross, He went to the Garden at Gethsemane to pray (Luke 22:41 and Matthew 26:26).

Jesus did this a lot. Jesus would go off by Himself to be with His Father, especially when things were chaotic and He needed direction, or when He needed to recharge His batteries.

Praying as Christ prayed is not the same as the human dance of conversation. You talk, I talk, you talk, I talk. No. It involves a lot of listening to things you can't quite "hear." (In fact, in 1 Kings 20, God's voice is described as a "still small voice.") You sit in total silence with your Father, without distractions. But silence is hard, especially since God is invisible and intangible. Frankly, it's easier to talk. But to talk through a prayer is a one-way conversation. Perfectly understandable. We humans are uncomfortable with silence, so we fill in the gaps with words like, "Lord," "God," and "Hallelujah." We also naturally skip forward, thinking of our next words so we sound good. But silence has a purpose—a valuable one. When we suddenly run out of words and rush to fill the gap, we're cutting off God's response. Just as God is getting ready to say something, we blurt out more words.

We never listen.

Stand in awe, and sin not: commune with your own heart upon your bed, and be still.

(Psalm 4:4)

How do you know that God is speaking to you? It's a good question. When you empty your mind, fleeting thoughts show up. How do you tell the difference between a fleeting thought and the voice of God? God's voice sometimes comes as a "knowing." It's a connecting point between the two of you that gives you clarity. Sometimes it's a whisper. Sometimes it's like screaming that gets louder and louder and louder until you can no longer deny it. You get the message LOUD and clear. You hear it in your soul.

When you hear the message, you can be almost certain that it's going to make you uncomfortable. Everyday stuff is easy. You would think of that all by yourself. God likes to challenge you a bit, to get you to reach.

I want to warn you, though, that sometimes the answer doesn't come immediately. Sometimes you have to wait.

And what happens if you ask a question and there is no answer?

So, the key to having a two-way conversation with God is meditation. Meditation is not sitting on the ground with your legs crossed and your hands in the air, exfoliating your mind of your next thought. It's simply emptying yourself. Instead of filling yourself with "self," let God do the filling. This is the difference between Eastern meditation and godly meditation. They empty and stay that way. We empty our core, and God fills us. God speaks then. With distractions gone and your mind settled down, God has the opportunity to speak, and equally important, you can now listen.

Sometimes the message is something that happens. It might be a person who walks by, a fish that jumps … that AHA! moment. Last year, we were all out at Lake Gaston one night, sitting around a campfire, yelling praise up to God. I was preaching, so I said, "Be silent and listen. Look up at His immenseness!" A spectacular shooting star shot right over our heads. It was God in conversation with us.

You can verify the message you get. Go to the Bible. The word *Bible* is Latin for *The Book*. (BTW, the first book ever printed on press was the Bible.) It was first called the Canon (not the cannon that fires cannon balls), and was used as a unit (or ruler) of measure: God's goodness and evil, light and dark, God and Satan. The Bible lays it all down. So when a thought comes, you have a unit to weigh out: Is it something God wants me to do? If you don't have time to search Scripture for verification, think about whether or not you would want this done to or for yourself. If so, the message is from God.

There is a story of a skateboarder. In the distance, he saw a homeless man sitting in his way on the sidewalk. He asked God what to do. "God, should I jump this guy in a spectacular trick? Or should I stop my board, reach into my pocket, and give him my money for a meal?" In silence, he received his answer. He received "knowing." He was clear which choice was of God and which was unkind.

Another one of the SouthTown team, Shawn, was driving up a hill when he passed a man struggling up that same hill in a wheelchair. Shawn heard, "How can you let that man do an uphill battle? Turn the car around, go back, and help him!" The message was strong on his heart. So, he did just that. He asked the man if he could use a little help. The man said, "I have been praying for years that one day,

someone would stop and help me. And here you are!" Shawn picked the man up in his arms and lifted him into his car, folded up his chair and packed it in the trunk, and took the man home. During that ride to the man's home, Shawn was able to share about Jesus with him. God had more in mind than a good deed; He was thinking of another saved soul.

Be still and know that I am God.

(Psalm 46:10)

... in quietness and confidence shall be your strength ...

(Isaiah 30:15)

CORE ACTION

Go outside to a park, to a lake, to a skate park. Anywhere outside. SIT. BE QUIET. When it starts to get uncomfortable, sit some more. Say, "God, I hear and I'm ready to listen." Sit some more. All of a sudden, when you least expect it, you'll know what to pray for. I hear things like, "David, your friend's in need. I'm giving you directions. When you've followed them, come back. We'll talk again."

Then, feel free to have casual conversations. You talk for a minute. Ask a question like, "Lord, what do you want me to do?" Then stop. Listen and wait.

Here's what I've learned about stilling my mind:

The question I asked was:

God spoke to me by:

This is what He said:

I knew it was God because:

Christy's Story

Danny and I met on New Year's Eve. I was at a bonfire with a friend and she introduced me to a group of friends, and it didn't take me long to see that Danny was the ringleader. His friendliness and outgoing personality immediately attracted me to him and we started talking. We quickly realized that we had some mutual friends and

Love is a powerful weapon.

Christy Tolentino

shared a love of the water. The next day I called up my best friend and told her I had met someone I was interested in getting to know. I wanted her to meet him but I told her to be warned he was not what you would normally say was "my type" ... if there is such a thing. I told her he was short, chubby, bald, and punkish. We laughed, but she knew by the way I talked about him that there was something different about this one. After meeting Danny just once, she confirmed that she too believed that he might be the guy I would love forever. She was right! I had never met anyone with such a dynamic personality who was not in the least bit afraid to go after what he wanted. He made me feel like I could attempt anything. We began spending more and more time together with a group of friends, which allowed us to get to know one another without having the label of being an official dating couple. There was no pressure. We could just be ourselves, but we both knew this relationship would one day go far beyond just friendship.

The Best of Times, the Worst of Times
Within six months, I was sure Danny was the answer to my childhood prayers. We were spending all of our free time together and life had never been more perfect. I had a growing relationship with Christ, wonderful parents, a great job, and a now the man of my dreams was in the picture. How could life be any better, and even more pertinent, how long could this last? I had heard my whole life that as Christians, we have to share in suffering and no one is immune from heartache, but I had never experienced any life-changing tragedy. Without meaning to, I think I began to equate living for Christ with enjoying a pain-free life. This fog I was living in quickly cleared two weeks after the best night of my life, for exactly two weeks after Danny asked me to marry him, my dad (who was the first love of my life) was diagnosed with stage four lung cancer.

YDLY!

You see, I am not only the baby of my family, I am also the only girl, and my dad and I shared a unique bond as father/daughter. He was my hero, the man who had all the answers and could handle anything. When I arrived at the hospital just minutes after the doctor had delivered the news of advanced cancer, I remember just knowing that I had to make it into my daddy's arms. That was a place that would be safe. The halls of that hospital seemed to stretch on for miles, but I knew if I could just make it to him, he would say something that would make it all better. When I did finally find myself leaning over the hospital bed and falling into my dad's embrace, he whispered four letters into my ear— YDLY! Those letters represent an almost sacred code shared between my father and me. When I was in college, my dad would write me a couple of times a week and at the bottom of each letter those four letters would appear. The first time I saw them I thought, "What does this mean?" It only took me a few seconds to decrypt the code. Those letters stood for "Your Daddy Loves You!" Every time I saw those letters I knew that everything was going to be okay no matter what situation I was facing. I knew there was someone in this world who loved me beyond measure, and this gave me the strength and confidence to be myself. My dad did a wonderful job of showing me a picture of what the unconditional love of Christ looks like. So, when I would return letters or cards to my dad I would sign them using the same code, but to him it stood for "Your Daughter Loves You."

As I spoke those letters back to my dad that day in the hospital, I thought to myself that for the first time ever I didn't feel like everything was going to be okay. His words didn't automatically give a cure to the problem. There was no cure to this problem. There were no easy answers and no amount of quoting Scripture or claiming promises could make the pain or terror go away. That day began the emotional roller coaster that would last for a little over a year.

My insides were constantly in knots because this was supposed to be the happiest time of my life. I should be care free—picking out flowers, tasting wedding cakes, and finding the perfect dress for our special day. Instead, along with doing all those things, I was having to watch my dad's body endure the damaging effects of chemo and radiation. I was holding my breath and

But, as all this stuff was going on inside my head and heart, life was moving on in the outside world.

listening with pure terror in my heart as we received report after report from doctors. Some reports would offer encouragement and others would bring devastating news that the cancer had spread even further. I watched my dad intensely and wondered often how he could be coping. He never complained and refused to give up hope. For years he had ministered to others as a pastor.

How could this be fair and how could he have lung cancer? He hadn't smoked since he was a teenager and had never spent even one night in the hospital until the day he was diagnosed with cancer. These were the human questions that plagued my mind constantly. I knew that God has a purpose for everything and that He promised to never send us more than we could bear, but knowing those things didn't replace the horror that I lived with every day. They didn't make this period of time seem like any less

a nightmare. I was experiencing true suffering, and my spiritual bubble had been burst. But, as all this stuff was going on inside my head and heart, life was moving on in the outside world.

My Dad Performs Our Wedding Ceremony

Our wedding day was quickly approaching and dad was surviving. It looked like he would indeed be able to perform the ceremony as I had always dreamed. In fact, my wedding day was nothing short of a dream. I was so thankful that God was allowing me to marry Danny and that my dad was able to not only walk me down the aisle, but he was also physically and emotionally able to walk around and stand before us as he performed the wedding ceremony. As he stood there with his head bald from chemotherapy and his body weak from cancer, he shared with Danny and me the importance of passionate love, strong faith, and lasting friendship. At one point in the ceremony, Dad joked that he had always told me there wasn't a man in America that was good enough for me. "So, what does Christy do?" he asked. "She goes and finds a man from the Dominican Republic!" The guests laughed as he added, "She always had a way!"

After lightening up the intense mood, Dad reached into his coat pocket and pulled out a silver ink pen. I recognized it as the pen I had given him on a special occasion several years before. I had the clip of the pen engraved with our special code. I couldn't imagine what he was going to do with it in the middle of my wedding ceremony. He proceeded to explain to our guests what the pen and the letters engraved on the pen meant to us and then in a surprising and totally heartfelt gesture, he handed the pen to Danny and explained that now not only would those letters remind me that my dad loved me, but also that "my Danny" loved me. There was not a dry eye in the chapel. I know what it took for dad to pass on not only the pen, which was a cherished memento, but also the emotional responsibility for my well being as he was unsure how much longer he would be with us. It was a more than special ceremony and a day that will be vividly etched in our minds forever. Stronger

Stronger Than I Thought
Another day that will burn eternally in my mind occurred just six months after Danny and I began our lives together. As it turns out, Dad's remaining time on this earth was briefer than we could have imagined. Late on a Monday night, I stood in my parent's bedroom at the foot of a hospital bed that had been brought in to make Dad more comfortable. Along with my entire family, I watched my Dad take his last breaths of life here on this earth. It was the most bizarre experience of my life. The thing that I was most afraid of had actually just happened. How could this be real? *Was* this real? I wanted to believe that I would soon wake up and realize life was as usual. Of course, that wasn't going to happen. Life would never be the same, but that didn't stop life from going on.

I remember when the doctors and nurses were telling us that he only had a couple of days and then eventually a couple of hours to live. I was so afraid that I wouldn't be able to stay with him when he died and I definitely couldn't imagine sitting in the room with his body once his spirit was gone. I would try to imagine standing alongside my mom, brothers, and family next to an open casket that contained his body as we greeted those who would come to offer condolences. I couldn't fathom that my legs would hold me up to do something like that … and all of a sudden here it was. The time I had been dreading and praying would never come had arrived. As my Dad gasped the last couple of times, I just remember yelling and turning into Danny's arms. I felt as if my heart would also stop beating. Then it was over, and I was still breathing. Not only was

I still breathing, I was still standing in the same room. The strangest sense of peace seemed to be present also. It wasn't like an "everything is going to be okay" peace, but it was like a "you can do this" type of feeling. I know that was the Holy Spirit giving me the physical and emotional strength to endure this time.

"you can do this"

Over the next weeks and months I experienced a rainbow of emotions on a daily basis. There were times that I felt like life was getting back to order and then reality would smack me in the face and I would realize that hey, my dad is dead! He is never coming back. Then a wave of depression and numbness would hit. One night in particular stands out in my mind. It was right before Christmas and Danny and I had been invited to a party with some friends. I had been looking forward to the party all week. I thought it would be a good time for Danny and me to forget about everything and just celebrate the Christmas season with our friends. I even went out and bought a new outfit. Then, when I got home and started to get in the shower, I fell apart. Danny came home and I was lying in bed crying. I told him he was going to have to take the nacho dip and go by himself. I even picked some kind of petty fight and used it as an excuse. Of course, he tried, but he couldn't fully understand why I was ruining what was supposed to be a fun night for both of us. I just couldn't do it. The thoughts of having to make polite conversation and act like life was normal all night were just more than I could bear. But then the next day came and the sun was shining and I had to get out of bed. Life had to go on.

So, how exactly does life go on? How are you supposed to put the pieces back together? That I am not totally sure about, but I do know that somehow I had to find a way to make peace with the fact that God chose to take my dad. I had to come to the place that even though I don't and probably never will understand why God allowed this, I still believe He is a good God. Even though He didn't answer my prayers for healing the way I would have liked Him to, He is still faithful. That was a conscious choice I had to make to believe that He is who He says He is, even when I don't feel like I believe it.

A Lesson in Trusting My Father From My Dad
I think about some of the times when I was upset with my dad because he had taken away something I wanted. Once, my dad made me break up with a guy just because he didn't want me tied down at a young age. To a fifteen-year-old girl, that's crushing, and I didn't understand why he would make me go through something that hurt so bad. But as I think back on that situation, I never remember doubting my dad's motives. I never thought he was hurting me out of spite or for any other reason than the fact that he loved me and wanted to see me become the woman God had created me to be. Because I was one hundred percent sure of his motivation, I obeyed him and found that I couldn't even stay upset with him for very long. I trusted my dad.

Now, I have to trust Jesus the same way. I believe His motives are pure. I believe He has a purpose for my life, and losing my dad was part of that purpose. Even though I am feeling pain now, He has my best interests in mind, and He is constantly shaping me into the woman I am to be because He loves me. Love is a powerful weapon. Love causes you to endure and hold onto hope. It is causing me to let go of my pain little by little because I trust my heavenly Father's motives.

In this life, I will never be able to fall into my dad's embrace and hear him tell me that he loves me or see those precious letters, YDLY, written on a note again, but I will continue to run to my heavenly Father and fall into

> So, how exactly does life go on?

> Love causes you to endure and hold onto hope.

His arms and trust that His love for me is as real as the love my earthly father demonstrated. I encourage you to try and do the same. Believe that no matter what the circumstances you are facing may look like, He is always at work. He hasn't forgotten about you! If you can't believe because you haven't made a choice to trust Him, please do that. He does love you. Maybe you can't feel it right now, but that doesn't stop Him from pursuing you or longing to come to your rescue. He is salvation!

If you are dealing with death or grief, please talk and listen to someone. I struggled with the fact that the Bible doesn't seem to give a clear roadmap on how to cope with death and how to deal with the endless range of emotions you will feel. My brother-in-law, David, pointed out to me that it is at those times when God intends for us to rely on each other and the testimony of others who have walked through similar circumstances. There is strength in numbers, and it helps to know that someone else knows how you feel. God created us with a need for human relationship, and I believe He meant for us to share in each other's pain and encourage when possible. I would encourage you to not give up hope. Keep trusting. The days may seem long and hard, but keep facing them one at a time.

By no means is my journey over nor have I become an expert on how to accept losing someone so close, but I am willing to keep experiencing life and keep trying. I am going to choose to put my hope in a commonly referred to truth from God's Word that also served as my dad's life verse that indeed,

"All things work together for good to those who love God and are called according to His purpose" (Romans 8:28).

You can have fun and be normal and still have God.

Jonathan Edwards, Age 15

**What a great gift it will be
one day when you turn to
your new spouse and say,
"I waited all my life just for *you*."**

RELATIONSHIPS

DATING

"Dating"—such a tricky word that has a thousand different meanings. To some it means countless opportunities to get or give free food and movies. For others it's a mystery that changes weekly. And while it's fun—especially when you're first starting out, dating is really a sort of hunt. You're looking for that one person with whom you're going to spend the rest of your life.

Early dating is where you make decisions about what you like and don't like in a partner. It's good practice for being in a relationship. But eventually, as you grow into an adult, dating will take a turn. You'll realize that you're searching for "the one." You'll get past the feel-good, butterflies-in-the-stomach moments that define puppy love, and move into a deeper relationship where each of you cares more for the other than you do for yourself. That's love. (By the way, when you find the right "someone," you can still feel good and have butterflies.)

And here's a tip. You can't change anyone. If you're dating someone based on his or her potential, and you're planning a complete overhaul in order to create a perfect partner, step back. This isn't love. It could be friendship, though, as soon as you stop planning to "fix" the person.

LOVE

When choosing the one you'll marry, love is generally the big factor in the decision. Love is more than a feeling. It's a choice. It's choosing to love someone even with all those imperfections. This is why we say, "Love is blind." It doesn't see the little problems; it sees only the potential.

The Bible talks about the characteristics of love in I Corinthians 13. In verses 4-8 it says:

"Love is patient, love is kind. It does not envy, it does not boast, it is not proud. It is not rude, it is not self-seeking, it is not easily angered, and it keeps no record of wrongs. Love does not delight in evil but rejoices with the truth. It always protects, always trusts, always hopes, always perseveres. Love never fails."

The description of love found in the Bible is a very high standard to follow! But what a wonderful way to look at love in relationships. You put yourself last and allow God's love to make your love complete! There are THREE of you in your relationship: the two of you and God.

VIRGINITY

When you're in love or even just dating, there's a lot of pressure to take your relationship to "the next level." It can be tempting. Making out feels good … and one thing certainly leads to another as if your body has a mind of its own. You can't help it. You know how to protect yourselves. You're alone. Only the two of you will know. It'll be fun. Who will it hurt? Sex will be okay, right?

Wrong.

Today the thought of two people waiting until marriage to have sex seems like a lofty idea that once was, but will never truly exist again. The media doesn't help much with the notion of the value of virginity. In fact, virginity is often a joke, and the virgin is depicted as a loser. We are bombarded with sex in every aspect of ads, movies, television shows, you name it—it's there! But the truth of the matter is that saving yourself for marriage is not just something that some old person thought of to keep people from getting diseases and having babies. It was designed by God for the protection of His creation!

So, what's the difference between having sex NOW and waiting until you're married? When you see sex in ads, movies, and television shows, you're missing an important detail: the connection made between a man and a woman when they are intimate. Intimacy isn't just physical; it's emotional and even spiritual. But when that sex happens outside the context of marriage, the partners aren't capable of experiencing all that it was designed to be!

Besides, God has said that He wants us to be married before we have sex:

> "Haven't you read," He (Jesus) replied, "that at the beginning the Creator 'made them male and female,' and said, 'For this reason a man will leave his father and mother and be united to his wife, and the two will become one flesh?' So they are no longer two, but one. Therefore what God has joined together, let man not separate" (Matthew 19: 4-6).

There you have it. God is telling us to wait until we are married to become one flesh. But how do we resist those urges we all have? Here's the good part. When God asks us to do something, He helps to make it possible. If God brings you to it, He'll bring you through it.

What a great gift it will be one day when you turn to your new spouse and say, "I waited all my life just for *you*."

CORE ACTION

Bring God into the relationship and keep Him first.

Keep yourself out of tempting predicaments. Name some situations that might cause you to weaken in your resolve. How are you going to avoid them?

Set boundaries before you get tempted. What are your boundaries?

YOU'VE ALREADY DONE IT?

But what should you do if you've already had sex? One of the greatest privileges of being a child of God is that you're forgiven. Go to God and tell Him that you're deeply sorry, that you made a mistake in judgment before you knew all that you know now. God has a way of making all things new—even you. So, you can start all over. From this day forward, you're pure in body. No more sex until you're married. Got it.

CORE ACTION

Ask God's forgiveness and ask Him to make you new.

Inform your partner of your decision. Before you do, how will you handle the argument? What will you say?

Go to the Core Actions of those who want to keep pure for marriage, and complete that journaling assignment.

PORN

Whenever we talk about pornography, some kids deny having access to nudie magazines and porno videos, and try to sidestep the discussion because it doesn't pertain to them. But the fact of the matter is that you don't have to go to "the dark side" to be exposed to pornography. Media gives us thousands of opportunities to be exposed subtly to it: in commercials, magazine ads, television shows, Internet, and movies … well, everywhere! Sex sells. And the fact that you're so used to it that you don't even know pornographic material when you see it should tell you that porn has already launched a dangerous sneak-attack on your moral code.

It all starts with a seemingly innocent little click in the head for sex. A passing thought fueled by a human's natural desire for sexual stimulation. From there, it grows until it becomes an ever-increasing addiction that will confuse your ideas about sex and love, and destroy your hope for a natural and normal sex life. Infected with perverted images, your view of sex can never ever be the way it's supposed to be: Pure.

What all this advertising and pornography *doesn't* tell you about sexuality is that love is a necessary ingredient for a fulfilled sex life. Love is energized by a relationship with the One who created sex. Anything less gives us false measurements of both good sex and true love. We get cheated big time.

It's easy to become addicted to porn. All you have to do is get a little TOO interested. The problem with porn is not just how it affects the person who is addicted. Unhealthy, over-the-top interest in porn is selfish. It does incredible damage to relationships. Maybe you are dating someone. How would that person feel if they knew you were secretly entertaining sexual pleasures that were meant to be enjoyed in marriage alone? And some that were never meant to be at all? Would they feel cheated? Betrayed? Could they still trust you? Would they fear that after marriage they would have to compete with the images in your mind?

Even if you're not dating, what about the guilt that accompanies this type of behavior? How does this secret affect *your* view of God's acceptance of who you are? Does it strain your relationship with Him? If you're sneaking and looking at things in secret, then you KNOW it's wrong. So does God, who, by the way, knows what you're doing and is waiting for you to stop breaking His heart.

CORE ACTION

If you are struggling with pornography, try the following:

Admit that you have a problem and ask God to help you.

Walk away from temptation. This could mean turning the television to another channel, deleting suspicious e-mail without looking at it, checking out a movie before going to the theatre, throwing out a magazine collection, or refusing to go onto the Internet when you are alone. Where are you getting access to porn? How will you have to adjust your life in order to avoid it?

Then find someone you love and trust, and let them know your situation. Make them an accountability partner. Tell them honestly if you fail. Let your love for that person and your desire not to be a disappointment to them be motivating factors in fighting temptation. "Confess your sins to one another and pray for one another that you may be healed" (James 5:16). Who are you going to tell?

Remember that Jesus is powerful enough to free us from any rope that ties us in knots.

"If we confess our sins, He is faithful and just and will forgive us our sins and purify us from ALL unrighteousness" (I John 1:9, NIV).

The 3 r's of the Bible:
Reading reinforces relationship.

At SouthTown we wakeboard for Jesus Christ and we show positive values. Sure, I believe wakeboarding on this team brings me closer to God and that's what is most important. And with God at my side, I know I will succeed. God is always here for me through thick and thin, and without Him, I wouldn't be the person I am today.

Kyle Ellerbrock, Age 18

The Miracle Over Lake Gaston

Meredith's family has been an invaluable support system for SouthTown from the get-go. The summer that Meredith's Uncle Robert and Aunt Lucetta suggested the use of their lake house on the North Carolina-Virgina border to have an overnight camp for their church's youth group, it was a no-brainer for SouthTown. So off we went, hauling our two borrowed boats and the necessary equipment.

A quaint cabin with a massive deck overlooking Lake Gaston was the perfect place for camp. The land sloped down to the cove where a boathouse and large dock were the center of activity: fishing, swimming, sunbathing … and snacking. A hammock between two tall pine trees was good for chilling. The boys set up tents for their sleeping quarters, while the girls staked their claim to the bunks inside the house.

The two boats ran non-stop from early morning to dusk. If wakeboarding wasn't your thing, the SouthTown crew was ready to give you the time of your life on a huge yellow tube. Talk about a rollercoaster ride! We must have bounced that thing eight feet high as the kids hung on for dear life, enjoying every treacherous minute!

As evening fell, a bunch of tired campers and their counselors gathered around a campfire that had been built near the edge of the lake at the bottom of the hill. It was very different from the busyness of the day. Mike grabbed his acoustic guitar and Meredith and Owen led some songs of worship, as all the neighboring frogs in the cove joined in with a loud and annoying song!
Some of us Riders shared stories about how we had struggled with different issues in our lives, including the very existence of God. But then something crazy occurred as David, SouthTown's pastor, started to speak. He began by talking about how the very creation itself speaks of the majesty of the Creator and praises Him. He joked about the noisy competition the frogs had been giving our worship leaders. Then he challenged everybody "to believe in the existence of God, if only because of His thumbprint on creation."

"Just look at this incredible sky tonight," he said as he turned to face the lake and pointed to the stars.

All heads turned upward just in time to see an amazingly bright shooting star streak across the heavens, leaving a sparkling tail in its wake. Everyone was speechless.

Could this have been a mere coincidence? Or was the very God of the universe so mindful of a small group of young people sitting on a patch of grass in front of a campfire one summer evening that He decided to give a private show of His awesomeness and power to reassure them of His love? Something to think about …

Believe in the existence of God, if only because of His thumbprint on creation.

How to do an Ollie

Set your front foot about four inches behind the front bolts and your back foot on the tip of the tail. Bend your knees and snap your tail and slide your front foot up to the nose of your board and jump.

How to Drop In

Place your tail on the coping and your front foot on the front bolts. Lean forward and push your front foot down, where your front wheels hit the transition. Then you should roll away. Leaning forward is safer than leaning back!

How to do a Nollie

Front foot on nose. Back foot in front of back bolts. Pop the nose, slide back foot to the tail.

Sometimes you're high above the water, sometimes you wind up underneath it, but the boat Captain is always mindful of where you are and ready to rescue you if necessary.

AUSTIN'S STORY

My parents have always led me in the ways and teachings of Jesus Christ. I've been going to church pretty much my whole life, which is just a few months more than seventeen years, and I've never really gone through a rebellious stage. Towards the end of my fourth grade year in elementary school, my family and I moved into a lake house on Lake Wylie in Tega Cay, South Carolina. I never could have guessed what a life-changing event this would turn out to be. I started knee boarding, skiing, and eventually slalom skiing. By the summer after 6th grade, I was on my first wakeboard. My dad would pull me behind our boat almost every day in the summertime.

There's a way to get over that emptiness that we all feel inside ... and His name is Jesus Christ.

Austin Hair

Meeting the SouthTown Guys

There is not much to say about my life before I met SouthTown. I first met Danny when I was 12 years old. My dad and I were out on the lake and I was, of course, wakeboarding when I saw another wakeboarder actually do a flip! I couldn't believe it! It was the coolest thing I had ever seen. I pointed my finger straight ahead as I shouted, "Dad, follow that boat!" So we trailed these riders around the cove, watching them do different flips and other fascinating things. Thinking back on it, they were actually probably pretty upset because of the extra rollers we were sending down the cove, causing them bad conditions for wakeboarding. However, my dad, being the aggressive salesman that he is, soon slowed them down to talk to them. Their names were Danny Tolentino and Andy Reise. They were really nice guys, and if they were irritated at us messing up their conditions, they didn't show it. Danny even told me that I was welcome to ride with him any time.

I was really excited about being invited to ride with the best wakeboarders on the lake, but also a bit nervous. I was behind their boat, the 2001 Nautique, and it was a hot Carolina summer day. The lake felt refreshing as I slid into the water with my board on. I was still really anxious about riding because I felt like I had to prove myself.

I felt like I had to prove myself.

When I got up and looked at the wake for the first time from behind the boat, I noticed how big it really was! It had never seemed this big when my dad and I had watched them from 30 yards away from our boat! I gulped as I stared at the monstrous vertical wake. The more I looked at it, the scarier it got. I cut out just a little bit and started to drift back in. Seconds seemed like minutes. As I got closer to the "Wake of Doom," I started getting really scared. It kept getting larger and more terrifying. I could feel myself riding up the wake now. I was getting closer and closer to the top. My board left the top of the wake and I closed my eyes as my heart stopped. Then it was over. It seemed like before I had ever even gotten into the air, I landed again. I looked around to make sure everything was okay. Amazingly, I was still holding on to the handle and everything. I then realized that I had gotten only a mere three inches of air. Well, after that I told myself I wasn't going to let that happen again. So I started doing bigger jumps and eventually brought out the big stuff that day. And by big stuff, I mean that I would clear the wake and maybe grab the board if I was feeling good. That was my very first wakeboard lesson with SouthTown, and would prove to be a turning point in my future as a pro rider.

Time to Get Serious

When Danny realized how serious I was about wakeboarding, he recommended that our family go to some INT League stops. INT League is an amateur water sports tour during the summertime that has competitions for wakeboarding, knee boarding, and slalom skiing. So as soon as we were able, our family heeded the advice and went to an INT stop. I competed in all three categories: wakeboarding, knee boarding, and slalom skiing. My little sister, Natalie, competed as well.

Slalom skiing was the first event of the morning. I was so nervous waiting on the dock before my turn. The thing I was most nervous about was actually getting up and out of the water. "Austin Hair," said the lady at the end of the dock, "you're up next." So I put on my ski and other equipment and waited for the boat to come back. I remember the water seemed so cold that day, even though it was June. I waited in the water as the rope got tight. Getting up on a slalom ski is a difficult thing when one first learns; I think it's a lot harder than getting up on a wakeboard at least ... Ready

"Ready?" asked the guy in the boat.

"Ready," I confirmed. We started to accelerate quickly. I kept my ski straight up and in front of me, and was able to get right up. I smiled as the first part of the challenge was over. I cut across the wake a couple times trying to get as many buoys as possible, but only getting 2 or 3, which I was happy with, being that this was one of the first times I was ever on a course.

It was at that same INT League stop that I wakeboarded in a competition for the first time. I was still nervous waiting on the dock before I rode. I didn't want to make a fool out of myself in front of everyone. I suppose the most encouraging thing was that I wasn't the worst person out there, although I was very close. I can remember getting ready while silently praying to God. I just prayed that He would allow me to ride well. Riding in a competition is totally different from riding at home because there's a lot more pressure on you. However, I was able to perform relatively well. I think I only fell once. I was also able to make it all the way down the course and back. I don't remember a whole lot about my first competition, but I do remember I was happy with the way it turned out and I had a lot of fun.

Danny's Idea Takes Shape

Although Danny, Andy, and Mike were great riders and instructors, and I looked up to them a lot, they weren't the best role models. One time out on the boat, Danny's friend was driving while Danny rode. The person didn't drive too well, and Danny got so mad, he was throwing his fists in the air and cussing at him. At the time, I thought to myself, "These guys can't be Christians." There were several occasions where I wish I could have spoken up and said something to them about God, or asked them some questions, but I never found the courage. It was about three months after my first ride with Danny that he called my dad and asked if he could meet him somewhere to share an idea. So my dad, Danny, and I went to the basement of my church, Lakeshore Christian Fellowship. Danny had come up with a plan; he proposed a Christian wakeboard camp. Here they would teach kids how to wakeboard while sharing the love of God. The first question that came to my mind was: How in the world did *Danny* get this idea? Even though I didn't know what was responsible for this sudden change in Danny's life, I knew it was awesome.

Wakeboarding Takes Off and Life Changes

The next year, 2001, was a really big year for all of us. SouthTown's camp was up and running, and I was a regular. I was 13 now. Mike Wood taught me my first invert, the Back Roll. I was riding behind my boat, and Mike would ride beside me in his jet ski and watch me try it. "Look up towards the sky more," he would say. "Make sure you keep your handle in."

After so many tries that day, I finally stuck the Back Roll. I was ecstatic! I couldn't believe that *I* had done a flip on the wakeboard! This was a major turning point in my riding that summer.

My family and I started looking into the future a couple months, and realized that if I was going to go to all of the tournaments, I was going to miss a lot of school. So we decided that I would be home schooled. I would do work for approximately three hours each morning. My mom, a math teacher, would tutor me in algebra, and any other subject where I needed help. This allowed me to ride for as long as I wanted every day as well as compete in tournaments. But with this freedom came a downside. Loneliness. I had a friend who I would ride with on a regular basis, but only for about two and one half hours. There were many times when I wasn't wakeboarding or doing schoolwork. I would be at home by myself, so my social life changed a lot. I didn't get to see anyone at school anymore, and not being outgoing, I lost contact with a lot of people.

Don't get me wrong, I still had some friends, but it was not the same thing as being in school. I think that Jesus kept me going in this time where depression was a definite temptation. I didn't really understand much about who God was, but I prayed daily and studied the Bible often. I knew from going to church that God could solve any problem and bring me through any dilemma. I relied on God to be my companion when I was lonely, and this made me feel so much better. By the time the first semester of eighth grade was over, I was ready to go back to regular school again, so I did, and with much appreciation, I might add.

Home schooling, however, did give me the extra freedom I needed to compete in tournaments. I was able to compete in the INT Nationals Outlaw division, the American Wakeboard Association, or AWA, nationals, and the World Wakeboard Association, or WWA, nationals. I got to the semi-finals in the WWA Nationals that year.

The next season, the summer of 2002, SouthTown's camp got a little more serious. The days were becoming more occupied with campers. We also started becoming more earnest about teaching people in the ways of Jesus. At night, after camp was over, we would sit around a campfire and either sing praises or have a little devotional. Every day would also start out with a prayer.

At the end of this summer I realized wakeboarding showed some real potential for me, and I decided that if it were at all possible, I would become a professional wakeboarder. I learned some technical tricks at camp that season and was able to apply

Have you ever blamed God when things didn't go your way?

them in competitions. I finished in fourth place in the INT nationals, and first place in the AWA nationals.

Sidelined by Cartilage, Gift in Disguise

In the winter of 2003, the pre-season, one might call it, I tore the cartilage in my knee. The cartilage is the tissue that keeps your knees safe and padded. This meant that I had to have surgery as soon as possible. But there was a problem. Surgery requires one of two things—money or insurance, neither of which we had because my dad had been unemployed for nearly a year. He had just started his own business, however, and after about a month and a half of living with this injury, I finally was able to have the required surgery. I would need over a month of recovery and it was already May, the first month of wakeboard season. This was such a disappointment to me. It pretty much ruined my whole summer. Have you ever blamed God when things didn't go your way? Well, I did for a while. Even though I tried not to let this situation get me down, I wasn't always successful. I distracted myself by concentrating on schoolwork and training my knee so it would be ready when I was able to ride again.

> I jumped on this idea like a monkey jumps on the bed.

One day I was just lying out on the trampoline, staring up at the sky. I was thinking about the setback my injury had caused, and ready to call it quits on the whole wakeboard thing, when my mom came outside to talk to me. She and my dad proposed an exciting idea. The world competition was going to be held in Australia this year, but I had to compete in the Jr. Men's division at the nationals in order to qualify. Their plan was this: I could ride in the nationals and then compete at the Worlds in Australia. Being that I lost a large part of my season from having a torn cartilage, they would find a wakeboard family for me to stay with and ride with while it was winter here in the U.S. That way I would make up the time I had lost from my injury. I jumped on this idea like a monkey jumps on the bed. I felt bad for blaming God too, because He had seen the bigger picture that I had not. (Trusting Him totally in every situation is one lesson that I would still not learn for a while to come. I know now that this is so important because He always makes things turn out for the best—like having surgery on my knee. Even though I thought it was a bad thing, He turned it into a great thing by letting me go to Australia.)

Time to Say Good-bye

I coached at South Town's camp that summer of 2003 before I was physically able to ride again. This was the year that SouthTown Riders wakeboard camp really picked up. Danny, his brother David, David's wife Meredith, Erin Easter, and some others now all worked for SouthTown full time. The Lord provided for us in so many ways. We picked up sponsorships for wakeboards from Hyperlite, the leading company in the wakeboard industry. Also, by some glorious miracle from God, we got a boat sponsorship, too. And not just one, but two boats, from a company called Supra/Moomba, or Skier's Choice! We knew that all these sponsorships were answers to prayer!

I started riding almost halfway through the wakeboard season. It took a while, but eventually I was back to where I was the summer before, and was able to learn several new tricks as well. I qualified for the INT Nationals in California, and also rode in the AWA Nationals, which automatically qualified me for the World's in Australia. The INT Nationals were held in October, one week before World's. So, since California is on the way to Australia anyway, I planned to leave straight from the INT Nationals and get on the plane for Aussie. I got second place at the INT nationals, an improvement from the year before, but still not what I wanted. After the tournament was over, my family and I drove back to the LA airport.

My parents had been preparing me for my departure, and I felt ready. I had everything I needed to go to Australia for about 6 months. Most people think that this would have been the hardest part, saying good bye to my family, but not for me. I'm not sure quite why exactly; it might have had something to do with my excitement for a new adventure, and that I could only look ahead of me. I would miss my family, yes, but I knew that I would be seeing them again soon. For them it was a different story, though. I could see it in their eyes. It wasn't the same as it was for me. My parents saw their son, who only weeks before had turned sixteen, taking one of the first steps in becoming a man. I looked at my parents and my three sisters standing beside them. They already seemed distant to me; it was like I was prepared for this moment already. We prayed together for all of our safety, and that God would bless me in my new home in a foreign country. My mom's eyes swelled with tears as she said good-bye to me, and gave me a hug. My father looked at me with a strange look at the time, but what I know now is a look of pride. He managed to smile for me as we said good-bye. I gave all of my sisters good-bye hugs as well, and then we parted our ways for what was going to be my longest period of time ever away from home.

Getting onto the plane it hit me. I was going to be on my own. I wouldn't have my parents to bail me out of anything. I was really becoming an adult. The flight was tedious, thirteen hours long to be exact. I managed to sleep for about eight hours, which was good because that would be the only sleep I would get that night anyway. As we approached Sydney from the sky, I began to recognize some familiar sites: the Sydney Harbor Bridge, the Opera House, and the tall buildings. This was not my first time in Australia. I had been here once before with my grandmother when I was in fourth grade.

Australia

The mother of the family I was staying with was to pick me up from the airport, but this was a problem. I had never met this woman before, and I had no idea what she looked like. The airplane landed, and as I got off I looked all around the Sydney airport. It was intimidating. I followed the crowds to the baggage claim area, which was chaotic. Everywhere I looked there were people from all over the world. After about two hours I got through the chaos and customs to find even more chaos in the pick-up lobby. I carried my backpack and rolled my heavy board bag and my bag of clothes, and searched the crowds for the woman I didn't know. After I realized this could take a while, I set my bags down outside, and then went back inside. I tried to look at every person to see if it was she, which didn't help because I still didn't know what she looked like. I began to get worried. My flight had been delayed a little bit; maybe she had left already and expected me to get a cab or something. Thoughts began whizzing through my head. I couldn't see straight. I began panicking. Then I heard heavily accented Australian voice ask, "Are you Austin Hair?" I looked up to see Brenda Harris, the mother I was to stay with, and her son, Cory Harris. Everything calmed back down, my thoughts stopped screaming, and I knew it would be all right.

It took about 45 minutes or more to get to my host's house from the airport. As we turned into their neighborhood, I saw houses that were different from any houses I had seen in America. Most of the houses were really wide and really long, but only one story high. We pulled into their driveway and I saw their massive house for the first time. I couldn't believe how big it was! It looked like a hotel or something. It was three stories high, and each floor had about seven rooms. I was led upstairs, which was where all the bedrooms were, and where I would have my own room.

Cory was one year younger than I, and he had a younger brother, Kurt. Their dad's name was Neil. Neil and Brenda were organizing the IWSF Worlds that year. We went to the tournament site the same day that I got there. They could not have picked a better spot to have a wakeboard tournament. It was where the rowing was held for the Sydney Olympics in 2000. The shore was lined with rocks, so there would be no rollback. It was a private lake, so other boats would be on there. Pretty much, the water would always be smooth. But the most original thing was the seating. There was a giant stadium with tons of bleachers that were all covered from the rain. The stadium was set up on the hill, so any spectator could get a perfect view of the contest at any time. This is a very important aspect in choosing a site for any wakeboard contest.

The IWSF Worlds
We went to the hotel near the site about two days after I arrived. On Monday people started getting practice runs for the contest. Competition was to start on Thursday. I got to take a lot of practice sets on Tuesday and Wednesday. Wednesday I got to practice on the official course. This means all of the obstacles were set up the exact way that they would be for the tournament. I rode awesome for my practice set, sticking tricks like Whirly Birds, KGBs, and Tootsie Rolls. I even did a Switch 360 across the slider. I was excited about hitting the slider so well because it was an extremely hard slider to hit and as far as I had seen, no one had really hit it well that day. Of course this was great, but it didn't count for the competition. But I figured this was a good sign of things to come. Yeah right!

The next day, I didn't ride well at all. I almost fell on my first trick, I came off of the slider early, and I fell once. But, what I did do was enough to get me through to semi-finals. In semi-finals, I started my first pass out really well, but I had one fall at the very end. Then in my second pass, I did a couple of tricks and hit the kicker, which I fell on. (A kicker is another name for a ramp.) I felt awful, sitting there in the water, but I knew I could still have a chance at making it through to finals if I could just stick the rest of my pass with one more big trick. I decided I would go for a Wrapped KGB at the end of my pass. A Wrapped KGB is considered a technical trick. I got up and cut out for my first trick: a Switch Scarecrow. Stuck it. I looked ahead of the boat and saw the end of the course approaching fast. I did my second trick: Toe Side Off Axis 540. Stuck it. I tried to get ready for the Wrapped KGB; it takes a moment to prepare for this trick. I saw the buoys marking the end of the course just feet away. At the last possible second, I cut in just to do a Blind 360 because I didn't have time to prepare for a KGB. I landed the 360, but I knew that if I would make it into finals, it would be by the skin of my teeth. They posted the scores at the end of my heat. I missed the cut for finals by half of a point on a scale of 100 points.

I made a lot of friends at the Worlds. I met wakeboarders and girls, including a beautiful girl named Trista, whom I would end up dating while I was down there. Cory introduced me to a lot of his friends, too. Cory, myself, and some other guys would hang out every night. It was an awesome experience.

After Worlds was over, the Harris family and I went back to their home. I was to stay here for another four months. The first couple days after Worlds, I began to get a little homesick. It was kind of like the climax was over for now. But that feeling quickly faded away as I became occupied in many other things. Schoolwork was taken care of through a laptop. I would spend about three hours on the laptop every day. The Harris family was really generous to me. Cory, Neil, and I took the boat out anywhere from two to three days a week. On the days we didn't ride, I would go up to the water ski shop that Neil owned and help out up there. I was also able to go and stay with different people as well. My aunt and uncle lived in Sydney, so I would stay with them from time to time. I also knew some people who were really good friends of my parents who I was able to stay with.

Lake Conjola: My First Saltwater Encounter
One of the most fun trips I took was to a place called Lake Conjola. There, I stayed at a lake house where wakeboarders, whom I had met, lived. It was a saltwater lake that fed straight into the ocean. The lake was absolutely beautiful. There were hardly any houses anywhere, so trees surrounded the whole lake. This was the first time I had ever wakeboarded in salt water before. It was a little bit different, but I was able to get used to it quickly. The guys were so nice for letting me go and stay with them. They were all awesome riders as well.

Christmas with My Family
One great thing that happened was that my mom and two youngest sisters were able to come to Australia for a month. This was wonderful because now I could spend Christmastime with my family. Shortly after New Year's, we all left to go back to America together. The Harris family had made it all possible for me. I would never forget this once- in-a-lifetime journey, or the close friends I had made during my stay.

Return to "Normal" Life in the USA
I got back home and went to school the very next day, just in time to start the second semester of my tenth grade year. Back in school though, I found myself feeling depressed, lonely, and stressed out. I asked myself, "What's the point? Why do I go through all this trouble?" There are so many things I am required to do. In high school, I go to school for almost 8 hours every day, then come

home and have more homework to do. If I want to stay in shape, I spend another one to two hours weight training or playing a sport. There are also extra curricular activities that I am supposed to be doing so that I can go to a good college. By the end of the day, I am ready to fall into bed and hope my dreams transport me to a place where my sleep seems longer. I do understand why we go through this process. I want to do well in high school to go to a good college. I want to go to a good college to get a good job. And I want to get a good job to make a lot of money. But then what? Is that my whole purpose in life? To make the most money I can for myself so that I can be happy? When I'm on my deathbed, am I going to look around and say, "Wow, I'm glad I spent all my time making money. Now I can die with a big house and a nice car?" Probably not.

Christ's Purpose for Me

It was during this time that I discovered real hope in Jesus Christ. I realized that if I know Him, I should be living for Him. Living for Jesus and telling people about Him give us genuine reasons to live and provide us with an eternity filled with happiness. That is the simplest way I can put it. Live for Jesus. It's amazing how such a simple statement gives a whole new light to things.

One thing that I have learned about God is that He is unpredictable. He has set up a path for us to follow, and there is no way that we can fathom why some things happen to us. The only thing I can say is that in the end, it all works out. God is everlasting, and He knows what's best for us at the time, even if we don't think so. Sometimes things happen to me where I am just like, "God, how could you allow this? What did I do?" But really, it's nothing we do; sometimes we just need to be tested and put through situations so that we can learn from them and grow stronger. After all, if it doesn't kill you, it makes you stronger. What kind of a Christians would we be if we never had to go through any hardships? Weak ones, that's what kind.

Competing with God in Control

This past summer I couldn't wait for the pro tour to start. I was really excited about riding in the Jr. Men's division. The only thing was that you had to place in the top 20 in order to continue on to the rest of the stops. Well, I didn't ride so hot at the first stop, but I did tie for like nineteenth place with 5 other people. So this meant that about 24 people would go on to the next tournament, but some of us would be washed out here. So I was like, "It's cool; God has a plan; I'm going to make it at the next stop." However, the next stop rolls around and I don't make it in that one either. I missed by only one position! So now I'm really disappointed. I'm questioning everything from, "How could God let this happen to me?" to my commitment in wakeboarding in general.

But then some answers started coming. My knee had been hurting, and it turns out I had a torn cartilage again and would immediately need surgery. Although this was bad news, it meant that I wouldn't be able to compete at the next tour stop anyway. So okay, I didn't ride well so that I could get surgery? Yeah, that is a much better plan in the end ... not. But there's more. By not riding the tour this year, I had a lot more time to ride at home and practice.

I have to say that I believe a real spiritual turning point happened about this time. I was to ride in a tournament in Texas, yet wasn't feeling very confident all. But for the first time ever, I think I really began to understand that God had His hand in all of this and that I truly could rely on Him. I prayed for His will to be done, and only His. Somehow from that point on, my riding improved remarkably. From here I made finals at Van Nationals in wakeskate. Then the following week I went to Chicago and won the AWA nationals in wakeboard and wakeskate. That qualified me for the world tournament in Spain. I won 4th place in the world and my team won the first US gold medal in wakeboarding ever!

Well, don't give up on God yet.

So everything ended up making sense. Do things sometimes not make sense to you? Do you wonder how God could let those things happen to you? Well, don't give up on God yet. After all, He knows what's going to happen when we don't. Stay close to God and persevere to the end because you'll probably end up finding out a reason for those things in time

It seems that just yesterday I was taking my first wakeboard lesson with Danny and could barely jump the wake, and now just a few years later at seventeen years old I have a world ranking. But more than that, because of South Town Riders, I am at a stronger point in my Christian walk. There are a lot of things that other teenagers do that I'm proud to say I don't do. I have learned that there are alternatives to partying, alcohol, and drugs. Take wakeboarding for example. You don't have to get high or drunk to have fun doing that! It's a lot of fun just to take a boat out on the lake and ride all day with some friends. And in the wintertime there's always snowboarding! It seems to me that sometimes partying is just a way to make one feel complete. There's a way to get over that emptiness that we all feel inside ... and His name is Jesus Christ. Asking Jesus into your life fills you with a new hope and compassion. Jesus can fill your needs better than anything else, and all you have to do is ask Him through prayer. Just try it.

You can only
truly know God
when you realize
you know nothing.

MONEY

The Bible mentions the word *money* more than 120 times (and this doesn't count *coins* and *gold* and *silver*), so we know that it's an important consideration and a complicated issue.

Although money is important, we all need to come to a point when we understand that we need nothing more than God, family, and friends. Get this. I'm not saying spending money is bad. But, really, it's not necessary to spend a ton of money, go out to eat every day, rent a movie, go to every new film in the theatre, and buy the newest clothes, shoes, and video games. True peace in life comes from being content with what you have. Paul says, "… for I have learned in whatever state I am, to be content" (Philippians 4:11).

A tireless quest for more only makes us dependent on money. Then our measure of happiness is based on how much money we have, which is followed by more work to make more money. When you're doing what you love, and content with what you have, then inner happiness is easier to achieve. Life is good. I have a roof over my head, food to eat, and friends and family who love me.

Next time you say, "I've got to have something," think about the difference that thing will make in your life. How long will it make you feel good?

I'm not saying this because I don't have any money. I have everything I need, and feel like I don't need to buy anything else. I don't have a ton of new stuff, so I don't have so much that there is nothing left to buy. Not too much. Not too little. It's a good feeling.

If anything, I will spend my money on someone else.

CORE ACTION

Have a good day. Take someone out to lunch, and you pay for it.

Who I took out:

Where we went:

How much it cost and where I got the money:

How the person I took to lunch felt:

How I felt:

What I had to give up to do it:

What I learned:

How to do a Nose Grab
Feet in Ollie position.
Pop an Ollie and make
your front hand grab the
board. Release the grab
when you are near the
ground landing on all four
wheels.

For I can do all things in Christ
who strengthens me.

(Philippians 4:13)

Inner-City Days

We were so excited the first day SouthTown hosted inner-city kids. I mean this is why we started SouthTown; this is what we had dreamed of: a chance to influence at-risk kids, the opportunity to share God's love with them. The ecstasy of the dream crashed the moment they stepped off the bus … actually one girl was chased off by another who lashed at her, pulling her by the hair, cussing, screaming, and threatening her. It was no longer surreal; reality set in immediately, and I knew that given the opportunity, these kids could hurt me, a female myself and not very much older than they were. I actually became afraid. But in my heart I felt the Lord assure me, "This is why they're here; this is all they know; now show them Me."

So we went to work, introduced ourselves and pointed out the boats they would be boarding. Most of the kids retaliated with shock and swearing, "I ain't gettin' on no boat!" Others protested, "I can't swim; I ain't gettin' in that water!" Most of them had never been in "open water" and some had never been on a boat: concepts I had a hard time comprehending, since I grew up on the lake.

After lunch I traded up duties and went out as an instructor. We spent the first thirty minutes begging for a volunteer to get out on the water. We finally coerced a girl into giving it a try. She stepped onto the back platform and said, "Now, this jacket's gonna float me, right? I can't swim." I assured her that the jacket would float and so would the board.

"You're going to have to trust me; I promise you won't drown. God's not going to let you drown," I said. She reluctantly climbed into the water. "See! Just like you're sittin' in a chair! Your hair didn't even get wet!"

She laughed and before she knew it, she wasn't just sitting in the water; she was standing on it! It occurred to me later what I had asked of her. I had asked for trust, something so easy to say, yet when I looked around the boat, I thought, "These kids don't trust anybody. Their own parents abandoned them to live in a group home. Their peers attack each other. How are they to trust anyone?"

Even if she hadn't learned to wakeboard that day, she did trust someone, and I think that must have been a huge step, whether she realized it or not. Yet she did ride, and she did great! When I helped her back into the boat, it hit me. It was the same girl who earlier had chased and threatened another girl this morning. This was the girl I was afraid of only a few hours before! Praise God I could see her through His eyes and not my own! I was able to brag on her and tell everyone how great she and the others did wakeboarding.

Every one of our instructors went home without a t-shirt that day because they gave their own shirts to kids. All we wanted was the chance to show these kids the love that so many had denied them, and God granted that wish. The majority of the kids got back on their bus smiling with confidence, having learned they were capable of something they weren't capable of that morning and having scored a new yellow t-shirt. We laughed; we shared; we loved on the kids; and another small part of our dream became reality that day.

What a great experience to find out that we can do more than we ever imagined as we trust Him as our instructor!

"For I can do all things in Christ who strengthens me" (Philippians 4:13).

CORE ACTION

Have you ever felt that God was asking you to do something that you have never done before? What was it?

Were you able to totally trust Him for the outcome?

How did it turn out?

Ask God now what He would have you do now. And when He opens that door and gives you that opportunity, do it!

But let's practice first. Practice loving someone "hard to love." Pick out someone at school or in your life with whom you don't get along. In fact, ask God to show you which one needs you the most. Make it a point tomorrow to speak kindly to him or her. Start small. Just smile and say, "Good morning." Try to see through God's eyes and do as God would have you do. Pray for him or her.

What did you say?

How did the person react?

Did your kindness change the way the person acted?

Could you see a little softening?

How much of the behavior you observe might be nothing more than defensiveness, hurt, or mistrust?

What could have caused such damage?

How much difference do you think a small kindness might make to such a damaged person?

What did you pray for?

What effect do you think your prayers have?

Heel Side Wake Jump

Come in with a progressive cut. Position your body as if you were sitting in a chair. As you start riding up the wake, begin straightening your back leg. Keep your handle close to your body and brace yourself for the pop. Once you are in the air, keep your handle close to your waist. The key is to make sure your arms stay close to your body. Do not let your arms extend out. Spot your landing and bend your knees as you land. Also, make sure your arms stay close to your body. If you do not keep those arms in, you will experience the dreaded face plant!

Can God give you favor with men? He sure did for me!

Jay Masanotti

Switching Tracks

Sometimes it's really hard to know what direction to take in life. It makes me think of the trains when I was in Italy. As soon as they pulled out of the station, they faced what looked like a network of options, even though only one track would be the track it must switch to in order to stay on course. I kinda found myself in a position much like those trains, yet lacking clear direction as to which track I needed to choose to keep me on the right path.

I was studying at Lee University, a Christian school in the small town of Cleveland, Tennessee. It was there that I met Meredith, although I was actually friends with some of her roommates. And it was Meredith who introduced me to her boyfriend, David, and that's how it all started.

Deepening Connections

My connection with David really came to a head when we had a class together: *Models of Youth Ministry*. Tony Lane, our professor, gave David the opportunity to speak in class about exactly what SouthTown Riders was doing, since it exemplified one of the five specific models of ministry that we were studying at the time.

Not long after that, Mr. Lane had our class over for dinner at his house, and that was when David started telling me more about the ministry. I was pretty naïve about action or core sports as they are now called, since I was at the time a "traditional athlete." So I just listened intently, and really thought that what he was saying was awesome. SouthTown had this huge vision, even though it was starting small, to reach out to all kinds of "alternative" cultures. They just wanted to tell those people around them about Christ. These guys were living it, so it WAS their lifestyle. I was hooked and this dinner was when the seed was planted in my heart to want to be involved in some way. I told David about my sports camp experience with Kanakuk Kamps in Missouri, and how I had always dreamed of working in a camp setting. It was after this meeting that God really started turning my heart toward the alternative crowd. He had to change my perception and attitude, because honestly, I thought all skaters were punks!

I thought all skaters were punks!

It was in the fall that I told David that I wanted to come check out the ministry for possible future involvement, so we met in downtown Cleveland for lunch and he interviewed me. I was freaking nervous—more nervous than interviewing with Kanakuk because I had no idea what I was getting into. I was really out on a limb too because I didn't really know David at all. After the interview, he said he would talk to his brother Danny, who was the president of SouthTown, and get back to me. I had already committed my time to Kanakuk for the upcoming summer, so we kind of left it at that.

Eventually I got word from SouthTown that they would love to have me come if possible and see how the ministry operates. So when summer came, I ended up working it out to have a week leave from Kanakuk to go volunteer at SouthTown Riders. I had already planned to take a weekend off for a wedding in Alabama, so I just added a couple of days to go to Charlotte. I was stoked to go and I actually made a couple of wakeboarding friends at work after I told them that I was leaving Kanakuk for a week to go to a wakeboarding camp.

I Try on SouthTown
My friends and family really went out of their way for me to make it to Charlotte that summer. My Mom drove me from my home in Atlanta to Cleveland, Tennessee to meet my friend Teddy. Then Teddy and I drove late into the night to get to Charlotte at like 1 a.m. Sunday night. Needless to say, I didn't get much sleep with the wakeboard clinic starting at 8:00 a.m. Monday morning! It was awesome though, because that day SouthTown hosted a group of inner city kids from a children's home and I had the opportunity to minister to them. The STR team let me do the rider profile at lunch, which is usually where one of the staff members would share about what God had done in his life to get

him to that point, and how he became involved with the ministry. It was pretty humbling getting to talk to those 20 kids that day.

I ended up experiencing the full gambit during my visit. They had a Bible study on Tuesday night and I got to encourage the team at the end of the meeting before we all prayed. I felt attached. I already found myself saying "we" and "us," even though I had only been there for two days. I also got to sit in on an elders' meeting that Saturday and see what happens on the business side of ministry. I wasn't a part yet, but it was as if God was giving me a glimpse of what would happen in the future.

Danny talked to me on Tuesday night after camp and said that he would hire me right then if they had the money! I knew in my heart that even if I didn't get to do ministry at SouthTown Riders, that I wanted to be doing something just like it- something on the edge. But at that point I was already committed to a year with Kanakuk, so it was all kind of a pipe dream.

pipe dream

Which Way is the Right Way?

Now this is where the track my life was on became complicated. I needed to make decisions as to the direction I would take, yet the road ahead was anything but clear.

The confusion started when the doors to do Kanakuk for a full year slammed right in my face at the end of the summer. None of the funds that I was supposed to raise were coming in. The staff informed me that they were releasing me from my contract because of the financial situation. My heart stopped. My stomach curled up into a little ball. I dropped to my knees and I literally cried. This was only three days before I was supposed to pack up my life to move out to Missouri!

But instead, I found myself back home in Atlanta. No job, no job leads, no desire to really do anything other than work at camp. I hadn't planned anything else in the ten months before graduating from college because I thought things were lined up. Yet I was left out to dry. I never had a resounding "NO" from the Lord when I was praying about the Kanakuk situation, and there were no other doors really open for me at the time; I had taken slow steps to walk through that door, yet it now had been closed, and I had nowhere else to go. I was stuck. I figured I had no choice but to try to make the best of it in Atlanta. I got a job working in the mall while I lived at home and tried to figure

things out. I was so ridiculously down that my lifelong battle with depression resurfaced.

Dealing with Depression ... Not the Right Way

My friend Roger let me move in with him and a couple of friends on the north side of Atlanta. It was a breath of fresh air, being on my own again, but I was still struggling with depression. I had a lot of time on my hands and I started to get into Internet pornography. I had been addicted before I was a Christian, and it had resurfaced while I was battling with this newfound depression. I didn't really feel like I had anyone to connect with in the house, so the porn was my solace. Definitely not a good choice on my part, and the next few months were an uphill spiritual battle. Then, by the grace of God, I started going to a really good church and got a good job managing a restaurant. My life began to turn around.

At about the same time I started talking to David on the phone. We caught up on things and I reiterated my interest in SouthTown Riders. He said that he would relay this to Danny and that they would be praying for me. Then I started talking to Danny, expressing my desire to be a part of the ministry. I shared with him about what had happened with Kanakuk, and how I got this job managing a restaurant. Danny just told me that they would keep praying for me. Even though I felt drawn to this unique ministry, I have to say I honestly struggled with the idea of giving up a thirty thousand dollars a year job to go work for nothing at SouthTown. So during that time I would just keep calling and checking in with the STR staff, hoping and praying for an answer and some clear direction in my life.

Charting My Own Course

In the early spring, out of anxiety and feeling like I was doing the restaurant job just for a paycheck, I started to force the hand of God with Kanakuk again. Have you ever found it difficult to wait on God for *His* answer? Well, I was really struggling with this, so I thought I'd help Him out some. I e-mailed my director and said I wanted to work with them again for the summer. So he gave me a maintenance position for a term. I would have done dishes at this point, I was so desperate to be at camp again. Yet as April rolled around, I could not get rid of the longing to be with the SouthTown Riders. It seemed like everything in life was teasing me with core sports. My friend Teddy had given me a couple copies of all these great Christian hard-core bands that I had heard on the boats at SouthTown and I was watching all of the X-Games coverage. It was torture.

Now I'm like, my heart is with STR, but I am not there and the door is not open, so I have my feelers out

Trust in the Lord with all your heart and lean not unto your own understanding. In all your ways acknowledge Him, and He shall direct your paths.

(Proverbs 3:5-6)

there for anything: military, other youth jobs across the country, etc. I was so confused. But then for some unknown reason in May, I kind of started feeling a peace about my future even though I didn't know what was going to happen. I started telling my roommate that I thought I was gong to be moving to Charlotte, and he didn't believe me. I got my taxes back at about the same time and it was a couple hundred dollars more than I expected. I'm thinking to myself, "This is a U-Haul and my first month's rent." I had also been in an accident that past December and now the insurance company was settling the claim by giving me a $1100 cash settlement. I had like $1400 dollars now and I knew it was my ticket to get to Charlotte and start my new life. I knew God would take care of me once I got there.

Saying Good-Bye to Atlanta

It was really hard to leave my restaurant job in Atlanta. Another manager left the same week that I planned on putting in my notice, and so it took me a while to build up the courage to tell my boss. I prayed about it for a whole week, agonizing over the fact that I didn't want to do this to him. But I just knew that my winning ticket had come in to move on. I wrote a formal letter with a month's notice, which went right up to the week I was supposed to leave for Kanakuk. Other than the money, this is where God totally assured me that STR was supposed to happen. Crazy confirmation came from people who weren't Christian, people who didn't even believe in God: my manager, another co-manager, and the restaurant owner. They all told me that they were happy for me, that they would give me their blessing to follow my heart. Here I am expecting chastisement, not their "as long as I was happy, they were happy" reaction to my resignation. "What?! Where is my manager? What did you do with the owner, God?!" He had softened their hearts and that was the final straw for me. Can God give you favor with men? He sure did for me!

I told my roommate, who was really upset about it, but knew that I had been talking about working in ministry for years, and he gave me his blessing as well. I was going for sure, and now things started happening to get me to Charlotte. In late May, my friend Kristy told me that her Dad had just bought out a business and that he could give me a job in Charlotte. So I had a job lined up before I even left Atlanta! God was setting me up.

Two weeks later, I left to do my term at Kanakuk before I could move on to Charlotte. That month was the worst time I had ever had in four years at Kanakuk, a place that had always been like Disneyland to me. I didn't feel like I was connecting with the counselors or the kids. My heart was set on STR, and I was in limbo with not really being there yet, but not living in Atlanta anymore. I

JAY MASANOTTI

felt like an idiot because I had pushed God's hand and it wasn't His perfect will, so it was torture. It was definitely a time of being chastised as a child of God. (But it was also a time of preparation for the things to come, just as managing the restaurant had been.) So after my Kanakuk term was over, I got my check, packed up my Civic and headed for Charlotte—"Charlotte or Bust!"

I rolled into town to live in the guest bedroom of my new best friends, David and Meredith, who were newlyweds. Within two weeks I got approved to get my own place, and was grateful. I already had a job, and now an apartment. I started working at the wakeboard clinics wherever I could be used. I had barely gotten my feet wet when a position became available to start working with the skate team.

"Ummmm, Lord, you know I can't skate, right!? Here we go!" Yet the Lord has been faithful to help me disciple this team and watch them mature in Christ, as well as in their athletic abilities. And as long as He allows, I will be happy to be a part of this ministry. I finally can say I am where I really belong.

**If God gives you something to do,
He will help you when you ask.**

Miracle and Lessons in Walking on Water

Jesus performed a gi-normous miracle. He fed a mountainside of people with a few loaves of bread and a few fishes, and even had a basketful left over. Most people—even the disciples—didn't realize that a miracle had happened. Only a small group of people actually saw it. After this miracle, Jesus decided that He needed time with His Father to think and talk, so He put His disciples in a boat and told them that He was going to send them out onto the Sea of Galilee ahead of Him. He explained that He needed some alone-time, and promised that He would meet them later on the other side.

The disciples left without Jesus in the boat. And He went to the mountain to pray.

They began rowing and a wind came up, so they had to row against the wind. It wasn't a huge storm. It was just tough. The Sea of Galilee is only about seven miles across. They could have made it in about two hours. But at the two-hour mark, they were probably only about halfway across. They were completely exhausted. Have you ever tried to row against the wind? Sometimes you row and row, but can make only a little progress. Sometimes you're dead in the water. And sometimes you actually get pushed backwards.

From land, Jesus could see His disciples straining. He could have done three things. Nothing. Or being the Son of God, He could send angels to rescue them. Or He could go out onto the water Himself. And that's what He chose to do.

He walked on water out to them. He intended to pass them by if they didn't call out to Him and ask His help. His disciples saw Him, but didn't recognize Him. They freaked, thinking He was a ghost.

Sometimes when things are tough, help shows up, and we don't even realize it because we're so involved in rowing … trying to get ourselves out of the situation. This is what happened with the disciples. They were so busy rowing against the wind that they didn't recognize that the person who could help them was already standing there—right in front of them.

Jesus said, "It is I. Don't be afraid." He didn't actually tell them who He was. He expected them to know. At that point, they recognized the voice they had heard so many times before. That's what He wanted them to do. He let them struggle until they cried out. As soon as He got into their boat, the wind died down. They were amazed. He had come to them at the toughest part—the fourth watch or about 2:00 a.m., at the darkest part of the night.

The reason He had let them struggle was to see how sensitive they were to the miracles of God. They had just seen Jesus multiply a few loaves of bread and a few fishes to feed 5,000 people, and yet it didn't occur to them that it was a miracle. In fact, they might not have even questioned where all that food came from. "For they had not understood about the loaves, because their heart was hardened" (Mark 6:52). But in a boat alone, struggling against the storm, it was just them. It was obvious to them that Jesus's walking on water and stopping the winds were miracles. Jesus wanted to put them into a situation so tough that they would have no choice but to recognize His power and call out to Him for help.

It's the same in your own life. There are so many miracles around us all the time that we take them for granted … like something as wonderful as breathing. God doesn't want us to be oblivious to the fact that He's all-powerful and doing stuff all the time. You can row all you want, but if you want to still a storm, you ask for help. When you cry out, He takes away the fear of the storm and brings peace. He wants you to ask for His help. Remember, Jesus intended to walk right past His own disciples if they didn't cry out to Him. He wanted their hope to be in Him. When you ask for help, you stop your own struggle, and put the problem in God's hands. He comes at the darkest part of the night. His true intention is not to walk past you, but to take you with Him, just as He took His disciples to the other side of a quieted Sea of Galilee.

Let me make sure you understand a few important points. God gives you instructions and then lets you do all you can do. He gives you a boat to row. "See you later!" Your goal is to get to the other side to rejoin Jesus. God sends you out alone to do that, to see how well you'll do it by yourself, to see how hard you'll try. You'll be the one rowing, the one working to get to the goal. But sometimes there is a bad storm. Jesus tries and tests. You struggle, and feel alone and afraid. But you're never out of watching distance. Even in the fourth watch, the darkest part of the night, He watches over you. Jesus steps in when you cry out for help, and the storm dies down. And before you know it, you've reached the other side, just as the disciples did.

Also you need to consider the possibility that struggle is your choice. If God gives you something to do, He will help you when you ask. If you're struggling, it's because you're still trying to do everything all by yourself.

Or perhaps you're struggling because what you're doing isn't God's idea at all. It's yours.

Another point is that when Jesus made Himself known when He came to the disciples, He said, "It is I." God announces Himself by saying, "I am that I am" (Exodus 3:14). In other words, He was telling them that God was with them.

Something else to notice here is that the disciples didn't believe that the figure standing on the water next to their boat could possibly be Jesus, because they had left Him on the shore, knowing that He was going up the mountain to pray. They were sure He would meet them later on the other shore. They knew that the fastest way from point A to point B was straight across the water, and for

God is always with me helping me along the way. As long as I remember that, there's nothing I can't do.

Jace Cooney, Age 10

Jesus to join them, He would have had to walk along the shore, or catch a later boat. They were totally surprised by His showing up when He did. And that's the point. Jesus meets you where He wants to meet you, not just on the other side.

CORE ACTION

Identify a project you're working on that has reached a grinding down point. Make a list of every single thing you've done to fix it ... and everything that you might do.

Take that list and throw it away.

Remember that you're never outside of watching distance. It's time to pray and cry out for help.

Now return to the project and know that Jesus is with you.

The project I struggled with is:

I knew the storm was dying down when:

Everything changed after I prayed. This is how:

Be different!
You have to
"breathe
slow" or life
will go by
fast and
you'll miss
your chance
to get to
know the
coolest
friend in the
world, so
"breathe
slow!"

Bob Bonds, Age 15

SALT

"You are the salt of the earth. But what good is salt if it has lost its flavor? Can you make it useful again? It will be thrown out and trampled underfoot as worthless. You are the light of the world — like a city on a mountain, glowing in the night for all to see. Don't hide your light under a basket! Instead, put it on a stand and let it shine for all" (Matthew 5:13-15).

One of the coolest things about Jesus is the way He taught His disciples. I love the way He chose to teach them. He taught through simple little sayings and stories with huge meaning and complexity. This isn't the common method we use in schools. This form of teaching allows the student more of a process of thought in learning. The way we learn our information at school is through a series of lists and facts that we write down, memorize, take a test on, and then right after the test ... forget the information. The amount of information that we retain is so little. Jesus chose a method that would cause huge amounts of disciple-teacher interaction so that Jesus could make a statement and the disciples would think and ponder, and ask questions. The teaching become part of their memory that would stay there and became part of the soul.

One of Jesus' shortest stories or sayings that He presented to the disciples and the people is that of Salt and Light.

Why Salt? Salt ... Salt ... As placing those little dots after the words, that's all salt really is. Little dots. Salt originally comes from the earth. It's not a new substance that has just been created, but in turn has been on earth since the beginning of earth's time. It's just fine granulated parts of a larger chunk of some part of the earth that has been excavated, crushed, and placed into a container, waiting to be used. Salt, just sitting in a container, has no humanly purpose. If you poured it out on your tongue, it would probably result in a disgusted look and certainly in the discomfort of one's taste buds. Only when added to something and then consumed does salt have purpose: to flavor! We place salt on food to enhance and bring out the flavor of that food. But can you see that salt? For example, when going to a restaurant where chips are served prior to the main course, as any good Mexican place will do, if you can see the salt piled on the chips, you might say, "These chips are too salty!" Without even having to put a chip in your mouth, what you see causes expectations of distaste and discomfort. Tasting the chips isn't even necessary to know that they are overly salty and aren't going to be good unless some serious salt scraping occurs before putting them into your mouth. But when salt is placed with perfection, just the right amount, on a bland steak, it combines with and chemically changes the composition of the morsel that is soon to touch the tongue of the consumer, bringing great pleasure and enjoyment.

Salt use can get out of hand. It can be so overly used that it can even become destructive. Large quantities of salt over a duration of time also have the ability to kill. Salt also has the power to destroy the usefulness of water. It can make water distasteful and disgusting to drink. It can almost become a poison to our bodies.

We are the salt. Our witness of Jesus is that salt. When we share Jesus, we are spreading the great flavor of the salvation of Christ. There is great responsibility in being salt. Don't over do it, where it becomes distasteful or poisonous. Don't attack people with salt. Think about why God chose "salt." In a strange way, it can be used for flavor, but *en masse*, it can destroy the food or drink. So add salt with care.

CORE ACTION

Have you ever gone too far and overdone it when you were telling someone about Christ? Did you lay it on so thick that the other person was turned off?

How can you give the same message, but do it so lightly that the person won't find you distasteful ... or worse, poisonous?

MIKE'S STORY

Looking back on my life, it really amazes me how many times it has changed dramatically. In middle school and my first two years of high school, I was awkward, a little lonely, and had trouble making friends. I just couldn't figure out why I couldn't fit in with the popular kids and why I couldn't get a girl to notice me if my life depended

> # You do not have to be in a ministry to be a minister.
> **Mike Wood**

on it. I only had one real friend at the time, but we had a blast together. It was kind of like that show, "Boy Meets World." He was the real popular guy in school, and I was, well … not. Nonetheless, we pretty much hung out all the time, playing ball, going to Hornets basketball games, trying to pick up chicks at Carowinds amusement park—just normal teenage stuff.

Moving to Fort Mill

At the beginning of the summer after my sophomore year of high school, my family decided to move about 30 minutes away to a lake house in Fort Mill, South Carolina. I was ticked. I had to change schools, leave behind the only real friend I knew, pretty much change everything. Though I started out mad about the change, I ended up having one of the best and most memorable summers of my life. Some kind of alignment of the cosmos must have happened, because suddenly I was "cool." I was THE NEW GUY, and the new guy in a small town is a great thing to be. Suddenly the slate was clean. Nobody knew anything about me, and in a moment I had more friends than I knew what to do with, and lucky for me, the kids I was friends with were really good kids. For the first time in my life, I felt accepted and loved. I started wakeboarding and jet skiing every day, and no matter what we did, we made it fun and exciting.

THE
NEW
GUY

Introduction to Christian Music With No Effect

As school moved along my junior year, I continued to meet people and make new friends. I play guitar and so some friends of mine and I decided we would start a band. We needed a place to practice and one of my friends in our new band had ties with the local community church. We were given the go-ahead to practice in the basement of the church, but with the stipulation that we could only play Christian music. At the time we where bummed about it, but we figured we would go ahead with it. As time went on we started really getting into it, and God started to really seep into our hearts even though we were not really in it for the right reasons. We started playing for the youth group and then performing for small youth gatherings. This is when our true immaturity really began to show up. A Christian charity camp invited us to come and play for their campers one weekend during the late spring. We went and played and it was good, but here's the messed up part: We got a hotel room and got completely smashed that night. It was ridiculous. We had the wrong intentions from the get-go and we blew it.

Even though God had started working on us, we were far, far away from being able to withstand temptations that came our way. The funny thing is, I don't ever remember thinking it was inappropriate. At that point in my life, it just didn't click. I had no real concept of what it was to serve Jesus Christ.

Nights of Partying, Days of Wakeboarding

As time went on, I left the whole church scene behind. I ran with a new crowd, and lived to party. Keg parties, smoke-outs, trip fests, and women became the norm for a good night out. This is when I started hanging out with the future SouthTown Riders crew. We all met by way of the lake and just started wakeboarding together. During the summer after my freshmen year at UNCC, all I remember doing was partying all night and then waking up way too early to the sound of a boat horn coming from the dock. That would be Danny and Owen making me stumble down to the boat, headache and all, to wakeboard all day, and they wouldn't take no for an answer. After that summer, I moved to Utah with some friends to work at a ski resort and snowboard for a year.

From Utah Back to SouthTown

Fast forward to January 2001. I had moved back from Utah, was still partying like a champ and, believe it or not, still wakeboarding with the SouthTown crew. We had, by this time, come up with the name, "SouthTown," and all wanted to go pro. We rode at least three days a week all winter long. It was so cold, but we were determined. On January 21, 2001 I was at a friend's party in Rock Hill, South Carolina. Danny and Owen had started going to church again, and invited me to go with them the following morning. I didn't really want to go, but I told them I would. Because I had to get up early for church, I only had a couple beers and headed out around 1:00 a.m. By the time I left, everyone was getting real tore up, especially one of my buddies, Jason. He had passed out on the front porch, so I carried him inside, laid him down on the sofa, and headed home. The next day after church I was driving over to my mom's house and I passed my friend Bob, who I hadn't seen in a while. We started talking and he asked me, "Did you hear about Jason? He's dead!" I didn't even believe him. I made a couple phone calls for myself and sure enough, he had been riding home from the party with two other people and they drove off the road racing another car, flipped several times, hit a tree and all three died. The bad thing was that everybody thought the driver hadn't been drinking, but his blood-alcohol content was three times the legal limit.

The Wake Up Call from an Amazing God

This was the wake up call of a lifetime for me. Although it was terribly tragic, looking back on this event in my life really shows me how amazing God is and how He will take whatever means necessary to get His point across. I can't tell you what that church sermon was about or what songs were sung or even what I thought about it all at the time, but I do know that as a result of this tragedy, God designed that invitation to get my heart and mind in the right place to see Him, to truly give up my old self, and to set my eyes on Him. It was around this time that SouthTown Riders changed course.

Each member of the forming SouthTown team had his or her own personal run-in with Jesus Christ. In a complex plan, strategically designed and customized for each member of SouthTown, God made himself real to us. Suddenly, once again, the slate was wiped clean. I was the new guy in a small town once again. There was no more playing in a Christian band by day and drinking myself into a daze by night. We no longer set our own goals of becoming pro wakeboarders at the forefront. We now had the vision of reaching kids through wakeboarding with the purpose of showing them the love that God has shown us, and hopefully help them avoid the extreme measures God used on us to get our attention.

Today

Now after five years of working in this incredible ministry, God has moved me out of the ministry for the time being. I have been working as a sales rep for a cell phone provider for the past six months and have been learning to be a good husband since I got married to my beautiful wife Bekah. Though my life is completely different now, I still see God's hand in my life and the lives around

me on a daily basis. I have truly been given the opportunity to be an ambassador for Christ to the people I work with. It was a big culture shock going from an environment surrounded by Christians and ministry to an environment driven by numbers, materialism, and dollar signs. Though it is very difficult to not have that constant group support for accountability, this time away from the ministry has really shown me that life is ministry.

The people I work with often tell me that there is something different about me that they just can't place. I don't say this in a conceited way; I only mean that God is using the values and morals He has set in my life as a follower of His Son to shine a light to my coworkers. You do not have to be in a ministry to be a minister, and though I often wish I could still be actively involved with SouthTown right now, I know that God is going to do incredible things with this ministry and myself.

MIKE WOOD

Worship isn't just what you do at church; it's your lifestyle.

When kids see us, they realize that it's "cool" to be a Christian skater, and hopefully they will follow God also.

Ken Harrison, Age 14

Letting It Out

"If I say, 'I will not mention him, or speak any more in his name,' then within me there is something like a burning fire shut up in my bones; I am weary with holding it in, indeed I cannot" (Jeremiah 20:9).

This has always struck me to be my theme verse for life.
That is, after I met Jesus, of course. When I first accepted Him, it was as if I couldn't keep inside me the great things that He had done for me. I had to let it out. I had to testify.

The context of this passage is a testimony of the turmoil and suffering that Jeremiah was going through at this time in his life under the rule of a tyrant king. So he considers the option of not even mentioning God to anyone anymore. The consequence is that his message, the story of God, is so intense inside him that it burns him from the inside out. To keep it inside is way too intense. He must let it out. It's kind of like buying a surprise present for somebody, and instead of wrapping it up and waiting to give it to them, you just take it straight home from the store and hand it to them in the flimsy plastic bag that the salesclerk put it in. You didn't even take the receipt out of the bag. It's that kind of greatness that God has placed in us. How incredible is it that His gift to us is eternal life! We can't just hold this gift inside us because we are scared of what people think. It has to come out so we can give this wonderful gift to others.

Over time, the fire inside us can get dimmer and dimmer the more time has passed since the gift of salvation has been given to us. It's what happens naturally with humans. We get something; we use it all the time for a while; and as it gets old, we use it less and less. The big difference is that salvation is not some video game that goes out of date. It's an eternal gift. It never gets old. All fires have the potential to get dim and go out. All fires need to be fueled.

How do we fuel the fire, you may ask? Simple. Fellowship, worship, sharing your testimony, writing your testimony, reading Scripture, meditation, prayer, fasting, loving one another, and serving others. Pain and suffering can even be fuel. Sometimes the most explosive dynamite is used when you pass through the toughest times in your life. When you come out on the other side, you can't help but let others know that God has taken care of you, and He has not let you down.

The fire is in all believers. Don't try and hold it in. Feed it! Let it out! Rejoice! It's this cultivation of the fire that gives you passion, vision, and purpose.

CORE ACTION

Think carefully about your life and all the ways God has blessed you. Think of where you would be without Him. If you're having trouble getting started, write a letter to God. Start it out with, "Dear God, Thank you so much for ..." It might be tough getting started, but your gifts are so great, it'll be even tougher to know where to stop!

Now, go tell one other person about your thoughts. Explain carefully what God means to you, and all the things He's brought you through, and all the things He's given to you. Try to express what it's like to be loved so completely by someone who would die for you ... and did.

(This is called your TESTIMONY. It's your story. Yours and God's. See the next devotional on how to give your testimony when you're witnessing to other people about God.)

SouthTown has helped me to see how wonderful God really is.

Scott Jones, Age 16

How to do a Pop-Shuv It-

Back foot: ball of foot on the side
 edge of board with toes hanging out.
Front foot: about Ollie position. Pop
the tail while pushing your back foot
 behind you. Pull your front foot up
and let it catch the board after it
has spun 180 degrees in the air. Land.

How to do an Indy Grab-

Have your feet in the Ollie position.
Pop an Ollie and pull your knees up to
your chest. Put your back hand
 around your back foot and grab
the side of the board. Release the
board before landing.

How to Form a Testimony

In a court of law, a testimony is when a witness gives evidence to confirm some event as truth. We have all seen this in action on many TV shows.

As a Christian, however, a testimony is a public profession of your faith. It's your personal story that gives witness to the existence of God. You give an account showing that God is real by sharing examples of God's actions or intervention in your life. It's the story of God's love, forgiveness, and grace, and is a way to share Christ with those who don't know Him yet.

Everyone who has made Jesus Lord of their life has a testimony. All testimonies are good testimonies! Just because you may not have been delivered from horrible things does not mean that God has not done wonderful works in your life. Not all people have mile-long track records, yet all are in need of the Savior.

Don't be frustrated or frightened by the thought of openly sharing your encounter with Jesus. Just follow these simple guidelines for forming a powerful testimony that will touch the lives of others and make them also want to know the Lord.

- Share about who you were before you met God and what it is like after knowing God.
- Include examples of how you came to know Jesus (through friends, churches, youth group, pain, suffering, joy, provision … the range of human emotions and circumstances that let us know we need God).
- Give examples of how you knew that Jesus saved you (peace, burdens lifted, a feeling of freedom from sin and being loved, etc.).
- Tell the story! Storytelling is what makes your testimony real for people. Make it personal and be sensitive to who you are sharing with, making changes accordingly. Help the person or group see that they are not the only ones with their current life circumstances and tell how Jesus got you (or other

believers) through similar circumstances.

- Don't be long-winded. You don't have to give every last detail of the chair you were sitting on when you received Christ!
- Keep dates to a generalization for they do not have as much meaning for your listener as they do for you.
- Do not to use religious terminology. This becomes confusing for people who have not grown up around church. For example:

"Saved by the Blood" — Even though being saved by the Blood is what we are, the general public will not understand. So in alternate words you could say, "It took Jesus being the ultimate sacrifice in death to allow mankind to be forgiven."

"Saved" — People do not even know what "saved" is, so an explanation will definitely be needed.

"Sinner" — Be able to answer these questions: What is sin? What does it mean to be a sinner? Can a good person be a sinner? Do you still commit sin after your experience with God? In essence, sin is anything that separates us from the presence of God.

- Do not be ashamed of what God has done in your life; nobody can refute your experiences.

There are three goals you should strive for as you share your testimony with non-believers: Connect with your listener(s), give account to God's love, and inspire your listener(s) to want to know Jesus.

These words of Jesus to a man he had just freed from bondage are still being spoken to us today:

"Go home to your friends and tell them what great things the Lord has done for you and how He has had compassion on you" (Mark 5:19).

CORE ACTION

Pray for God to give you boldness to testify to those around you who do not know Him.

Make a list of your friends who do not know Christ. Pray for the opportunity to share your testimony with them.

Ask God to give you wisdom and compassion as you tell them of what Jesus has done for you.

My goal as a boarder is to learn grabs and flips. My goal as a Christian is to pass the word of the Lord to other people.

Jerrica Decker, Age 16

Pictured here are the SouthTown teams: Office, Skateboard and Wakeboard.

From the front: Austin Hair, Danny Tolentino, David Tolentino, Erin Easter, Meredith Tolentino, Ruggy Ahumada, Jay Masanotti, Andy Riese, Troy Ogburn, Lauren Hustad, Jace Cooney, Al Gordon, Kristin Mayhall, Taylor Hoynacki, Bob Bonds, Jonathan Edwards, Kyle Ellerbrock, Max Drummond, Tim Holford, Andrew Smith, Austin Parker, Matt Hemric, Gage Thompson, Ryan Gustafson, Nathan Abplanalp, and Ian Counts. Not Pictured: Becky Bernier, Josiah Fahey, Nolan Galleshaw, Adam Greer, Ian Mosley, Chris Sheets, Christy Tolentino, and Mike Wood.

We thought you would like to see the level of commitment of the SouthTown Riders.

On the following pages, you will see the "contract" we give each team member.

Mission Statement

We have a threefold mission:

1. To make contact with the youth of today who are searching for purpose and meaning in life through the medium of action sports and music. We strive to guide each youth to find that purpose and meaning through the life of Jesus Christ and the teachings found in the Bible.
2. To encourage the church body in the areas of discipleship, evangelism, and worship.
3. To infiltrate the professional action sports realm by means of setting fundamental examples of Jesus Christ and representing the sports in excellence.

**Submit to one another
out of reverence for Christ.**

Ephesians 5:21

SOUTHTOWN RIDERS, INC

FYI

Contract

SouthTown Riders, Inc. is excited about the fact that you have this contract in your hands. The Lord God Almighty has a great plan for everyone of ours lives, and His will be done, that plan includes your involvement with our ministry team.

The SouthTown Riders (STR) team is just that—a ministry. We adhere to biblical teachings from Holy Scripture, and to the mission statement and beliefs of SouthTown Riders, Inc. as a whole. This mission statement is the very essence of SouthTown. It is enclosed in this contract. Please, read it carefully to make sure that it is the also the calling of your heart to engage in this type of ministry. It is not for all, and we do not boast in ourselves because we are a part of such a dynamic project. Rather, we humbly boast in the God who would allow us to join him in His work on earth.

We at SouthTown have found that we must make the expectations clear as to what we ask of you as a member of the skate team. We have done just that in the following few pages. Again, please carefully read to make sure that this contract is confirmed in your heart by the Holy Spirit. We do expect excellence in everything we pursue. There will be obligations, but just like any other sports teams, you are willingly committing to such obligations. If you cannot fulfill your commitment to SouthTown, then please do not hinder the team. It is a waste of your time, as well as the time of so many volunteers and staff at STR.

With all of that being said, we truly are excited that you want to join the team at SouthTown. We have a lot of fun as we learn and grow in the Lord together. We look forward to spending this next year growing in wisdom, stature, knowledge, and favor with God and with man together. May the Lord continue to bless you and keep you in the coming year.

Sincerely,
The SouthTown Riders

One-Year Team Contract
My Commitment to Serve

I now receive from SouthTown Riders, Inc. an appointment to serve Christ as a member of the SouthTown Riders Team from January (day and year), until January (day and year), at which time I may consider reappointment to another year.

As a member of SouthTown Riders, I will understand and abide by the following guidelines:

1. Ministry is our priority, not our own glory.
2. I am a representative of SouthTown Riders. This is a professional job; therefore each member and I will act in a professional manner at all times.
3. I am an ambassador of God, through Christ Jesus, and SouthTown Riders as a team member. My actions will reflect my relationship with and respect for Him. (Colossians 3:17/2 Corinthians 5:20a)
4. I will give of my best at all times in the service I have accepted. I understand that it is not ability or qualifications, but faithfulness to my assigned task that is of supreme importance.
5. I understand that it is my responsibility to be at each SouthTown event where participation from the team is mandatory.
6. When asked to do a task by leadership, no matter what the task, I will do it without question.
7. If there is something that needs to be done, I will do it. This ministry is mine also. I will take ownership and be excellent.
8. If there is a slacker, I will pick up their slack and THEN report the situation to management.
9. If I have a question or problem, I will consult someone in a leadership/authority position for the answer.
10. The day is not over until everything is done and I have double-checked the task list.

11. Malicious sarcasm is not an option between myself and my team members. We are a team, a family, and we don't cut each other down with the intention to hurt.
12. If at any time I am unable to fulfill such requirements of SouthTown, whether physical or spiritual, I will be a man/woman of integrity and I will address the situation with the Team Manager. At that time, appropriate actions will be taken for the good of myself and the team
13. I affirm the statements of belief of the SouthTown Riders mission statement and will conduct myself in such a manner as to glorify God through said statement.
14. I understand that it is my obligation to fundraise $_____ as a member of the team.

On behalf of the SouthTown Riders Board

Date:_____

_____ Team Member

_____ Team Manager

Overview of STR Team

1. Expectations:

STR is a ministry that is approached on a daily basis for involvement in a world of activities ranging from skate demos to youth ministry outreach, school functions to community events. We are very careful in what we obligate ourselves to because time is often limited and the work is often strenuous and time consuming.

Therefore, STR expects that the members of its teams will be at each event. Examples of such events in the past have been as follows:
  a. **Practices**: Team practices are held monthly throughout the year. They are usually scheduled for every other Saturday (two a month).
  b. Practices are often arranged around events and are strategically placed throughout the month to avoid burnout. In other words, if there are two big events in one month, then there will probably only be one practice.
  c. **Demos**: Reaching and impacting youth is one of our core beliefs and is stated in our Mission Statement. We regularly perform demos in the community as a form of outreach. These events are scheduled throughout the year.
  d. **Trips**: We believe in the power of fellowship with other believers. There is no other single way for our team to get to know each other than to spend time together. One of the ways we accomplish this is to pull the team out of their usual environments. We plan on doing more of the same this year, and hopefully bigger and better. **Costs for such trips will be covered in our fundraising efforts.**
  e. **Bible study**: This is foundational for a ministry to grow and to be truly impacted by the life of Christ. We will meet weekly to explore and grow in God's word together. Each member should have and bring a Bible to studies.

We have a very busy and exciting year ahead of us. As a team member, upon the signing of your contract, you are obligated to attend each SouthTown event. There will be no excuse for absence from events as they will be made known to you far in advance. We would also expect you to make any schedule conflicts known to us with sufficient notice, not the day before or of the event.

In the case of emergency, it will be your responsibility to contact the Team Manager, or another member of SouthTown leadership, to make known the details of your situation. A list of SouthTown leadership will be made available to you.

2. Behavior:

SouthTown is a professional business and should expect its members to act professionally. This by no stretch of the imagination does not mean that we do not have fun with what we do. However, our actions reflect on many other individuals and can either glorify them or shame them. These individuals include:
- God
- SouthTown Riders
- Our families
- Corporate sponsors
- Ourselves

SouthTown understands that conflicts often arise when a group of *individuals* spends long periods of time together in a *group*. We will spend long periods of time together, so we need to understand how to resolve conflict when it arises:

Conflict resolution process:
- All issues and conflicts should first and foremost be taken to prayer!
- Check **your** heart and motives in the matter.
- Any issues with another person on the team should only be discussed between the parties involved. Bringing other people into the situation is a sin. Hold your tongue—don't be a gossip.
- If the conflict or issues is not resolved in steps 1-3, take the situation to the Team Manager or another member of STR leadership.

If there is such behavior that is deemed inappropriate, then this will be addressed and handled accordingly and may include probation, or in some cases, expulsion from the team.

3. Probation Terms

The following is a list of punishments/consequences for actions that will **not** be tolerated by STR:

Probation with restoration terms:
- Actions that warrant probation (regardless of place, time or manner):
    1. Fornication (sexual immorality)
    2. Use of tobacco products
    3. Pornography
    4. Thievery
    5. Assault
    6. Use of illegal drugs/ Drug abuse
    7. Blasphemy (God's name in vain)
    8. Use of alcohol (under 21); irresponsible use of alcohol (over 21)
    9. Not adhering to the 10 Commandments, as written in Exodus 20:3-20

Penalties warranted from the above actions:
- First warning: 30 day probation period, pending involvement on the team, with option to resign from the team
- Member will be expected to attend all activities during probation period to support team without participating
- Must make public apology for conduct to SouthTown Riders Team

Grounds for immediate expulsion:
Endangering the life of a team member or student

Tardiness:
Excessive tardiness/absenteeism is unacceptable, and will result in pending involvement on the team.

Be imitators of God,
therefore, as dearly loved
children (Ephesian 5:1).

Devotionals are excerpted from sermons by David Tolentino.

Student quotes are by members of the STR Wakeboard and Skateboard Teams.

Downtown photos taken by Preston West and David Tolentino.

Acknowledgements

We want to express our immeasurable appreciation to the souls who were there before the dream was even a dream and stayed with us even through the high and low times, as we are forever indebted to you for your prayers, love, and encouragement.

First and foremost, we want to thank our Lord and Savior, Jesus Christ, for without Him, we are nothing.

Then to our Families, especially our parents: Phyllis Baker, Mike & Darlene Easter, David & Cynthia Hair, Donald and Carolyn Kinney, Pedro & Sally Tolentino for all you do....we do not even have words to express how grateful we are to each of you.

In loving memory of Rev. Richard Baker

We thank our Advisory Board: Donald Kinney, Russell DeShields, Tom O'Boyle, Phil Blaschke, and Evan Albertyn as they have and continue to guide us in our decisions.

A special thanks to...Ruggy Ahumada, Rodney Ashby, Jenna Atkinson, Brian Baker & Family, Rick Baker & Family, Darryl Bego & The Carolina Youth Commission, Becky Bernier, Eddie Beverly, Jessica Boulware, Kevin & Kim Brooks, Bev Browning, Ryan & Becca Cates, Robert Caudle, Ben & Jessica Cerullo, Jason Channell, Heather Cleevely, Mr. Cliff, Dr. Paul & Darlia Conn, Kevin Conway, Rev. Joseph Henry Cortese, Scott Costner, C I W, Dr. Datte, Chad Deal, Billy Dean, Kevin DeShields, Max Drummond, Josiah Fahey, Steve & Carmen Fee, Trevor Greer, Brett Hart, Greg Hart, Teddy Hart, The Hair Family, Suzanne Hamid, Bryce Hoover, Eric, Becky, Ethan and Annie Hovda, Dr. Jaber, Mr. Jasso, Nick Knieriem, Tony Lane, Chih-hua Liang, Lori at Ike's Skate Shop, Ma & Pa, Skip MacMillan, Beau & Monica Markolf, Jonathan & Amanda Martin, Billy & Julie Mauldin, Rachel Merchand, James Metcalf, Stephen Morrison, Tim Morrison, Old Bible Study, Pastor Roselen, Dario & Diana, Red Letter Seven, Shawn Redmond, Tim & Julie Richardson, Andy Riese, Chris Sheets, Jack & Gail Smith, Bryan Smerdon, Daryl Sutherland, Jacque Thomas, Trey Tiller, Jenneane Tillman, Scott Tollett, Ashley Tison, Mike and Angela Volpe, Lorraine Wallace, Jay Warren, Dr. Chris Williams, Cory Worf, Jason York, and Robert & Lucetta Zaytoun.

We also thank all the Churches, Volunteers, Friends, Donors and all our students from day one until now.

We thank you because your belief in this mission has blessed our lives and we are grateful to each of you.

A special thanks to all our
sponsors, who assist in making
SouthTown Riders a reality.

Ebenezer

Hyperlite
WAKEMFG

MOOMBA
TOURNAMENT INBOARD BOATS

National
RV Rentals
Inc.

Nitro-life
Films

PRO TEC.

Stateline
Skate Park

steelroots

SUPRA
LUXURY INBOARD BOATS

WESTPORT
MARINA
we sell fun!

If you have been touched
by any of our stories or
devotionals, we want to
hear your stories, too.
Please contact us at
www.southtownriders.com